DUCHY COLLEGE
LIBRARY

D1510526

Job hunting after university or college

The Transferable and Learning Skills Series

Series editors:

Anne Hilton, Manager, Student Learning Development Centre, Library, De Montfort University
Sue Robinson, Editor, Student Learning Development Centre, Library, De Montfort University

Job hunting after university or college, Jan Perrett
Research skills, Brian Allison, Tim O'Sullivan, Alun Owen, Arthur Rothwell, Jenny Rice, Carol Saunders
Successful group work, Simon Rogerson, Tim O'Sullivan, Jenny Rice, Carol Saunders

THE TRANSFERABLE AND LEARNING SKILLS SERIES

Job hunting after university or college

CVs and application forms
Being interviewed
Second interviews
Jan Perrett

**KOGAN
PAGE**

First published in 1996

Apart from any fair dealing for the purposes of research or private study, or
criticism or review, as permitted under the Copyright, Designs and Patents Act
1988, this publication may only be reproduced, stored or transmitted, in any form
or by any means, with the prior permission in writing of the publishers, or in the
case of reprographic reproduction in accordance with the terms of licences issued
by the copyright Licensing Agency. Enquiries concerning reproduction outside
those terms should be sent to the publishers at the undermentioned address.

Kogan Page Limited
120 Pentonville Road
London N1 9JN

650.14 PER

© De Montfort University, 1996

British Library Cataloguing in Publication Data
A CIP record for this book is available from the British Library
ISBN 0 7494 1869 9

Design and typesetting by Paul Linnell, De Montfort University
Printed and bound in Great Britain by Biddles Ltd, Guildford and King's Lynn

Contents

Part A: CVs and application forms

Introduction

This part aims to provide an introduction to the basics of written applications, to enable students to make the most effective use of the three main marketing tools: the application form, the curriculum vitae and the covering letter. It will also address the underlying need for self-awareness and job analysis.

If you have not completed graduate application forms before or if this is your first attempt at a CV, *don't worry* – this is a skill which can be learned and, once learned, will be useful to you throughout your future career.

Objectives

At the end of the exercises in Part A, you should be able to:
- recognise and understand the different usages of the application form and curriculum vitae;
- apply the principles of self-assessment and job assessment to any application;
- design and organise a good curriculum vitae and understand the benefits of updating it;
- complete a standard application form;
- compose an appropriate covering letter.

This book is designed to enable you to work at your own pace and, although each part is written as a complete unit, you may select the sections or exercises most appropriate for you at any given time.

Throughout Part A you will be presented with information about the process of making applications and will be questioned to check your understanding. You will perform exercises as you go through the text, including compiling a practice CV, which will form the basis of your own CV for present use and for future reference.

Good luck!

1 Self-marketing

Since you've picked up this book, I assume you're thinking of making an application for something. Whether it's a job or a postgraduate course, your objective is the same – through that application you will get what you want! But before you put pen to paper, there are some important things to think about.

Application = marketing

So what are we marketing here? Right – it's you. You are selling yourself and if you don't want to end up in the end-of-season bargain basement, you have to use a strategy.

Consider the following assumptions:
- I have qualifications from my university/college, therefore employers know my capabilities.
- I have spent several years in higher education, so I deserve a good job.
- If I give details of my courses and qualifications, that's enough.
- Selection is so hit-and-miss, there's no point trying to tailor my application.
- Every accountancy job is the same, so I can send the same standard form to loads of firms. I haven't got time in my final year to spend hours on applications.

You probably feel that several of these statements come close to the truth; you may even agree wholeheartedly with some of them. But they skirt around the main issue, which is that getting a job is your responsibility – very rarely can anyone do it for you (unless you're very well connected! *Giz a job!*). So it's in your interests to look seriously at the two most important aspects of preparing to sell yourself:
- *self-assessment*
- *job analysis*

This section of the book will get you started and tell you where to go to get further help.

Self-assessment

The instant reaction from most people to this subject is 'Oh no, not those questions again like "What are you good at?" or "Where do you see yourself in 10 years' time?" and the endless questionnaires which give a picture of your personality and values in just 20 minutes.'

This cynical response to self-assessment can be due to the way it is presented. Often it isn't linked to anything else, so you come away thinking – I'm a "social" person who values independence, variety and status (join the club!) – so what?' Or, because the

2

whole idea of analysing your skills, interests, values and personality is so alien to our natural reserve (you must never talk about yourself), you push it away with distrust.

However, selectors do need to see some glimpses of your abilities and personal qualities in your application. How can you answer a question like this, from the Marks & Spencer form, without giving some thought to your personality and behaviour?

'Give an example of where others have disagreed with your views (or you with theirs). How did you deal with this and what was the result?'

No? You're not interested in retail management anyway are you? (Coward!) Well, what about this one from a recent Lloyds bank form?

'What have been the most important events in your life so far? Explain what happened and why they are of significance.'

So you don't feel you're suited to finance either! You can't keep running away from these questions. Wherever you turn, you will find a similar one. Whatever you feel about the employers who use these questions, you've still got to fill in the forms, so try to be positive about it.

One way of being positive is to understand what the selector is looking for. In most cases they are not judging your answer on the facts, but rather on the way you use the facts to show skills and personal qualities. So you can see that knowing yourself is the only way you can come up with the goods. Well, you could take on another persona (maybe your best friend's), but it would be very difficult to sustain this through an application form, aptitude tests and two interviews! Anyway, you're not that bad, are you?

Skills and personal qualities

Most selectors have a clear idea of the skills needed for a job and also a checklist of desirable personal qualities. Some of these lists have been written down and you can find examples in your Careers Advisory Service (CAS) (see Chapter 4, Bibliography, page 37).

 Activity 1.1

Let's take a typical graduate 'management' position – don't worry about the details. What skills and personal qualities do you think you need to present?

I bet you had 'communication skills' – everybody gets that one!

If you struggled with this exercise, it's probably because you haven't got the vocabulary yet. You may know what you're good at, or what your strengths are, but not be able to give them a 'name'.

Have a look at this typical list and cross check it with your own list. Don't assume that this is an exhaustive list and don't assume that you have to have all these skills – that would really make a nonsense out of the selection process.

a **Communication skills** – the ability to communicate both verbally and in writing. Being able to express ideas in a clear, positive and appropriate way.

b **Problem solving** – a capacity for analytical thought and the application of this process to problems. Evidence of the identification of key issues and priorities.

c **Leadership** – the effective organisation of people and events. This will include some evidence of developing and channelling the ideas and potential of others.

d **Flexibility** – the ability to adapt to changing circumstances. A proactive approach may be sought, which also checks out *initiative* and *motivation*.

e **Planning and organisation** – the ability to produce logical action plans and to follow them through with appropriate strategies to a successful outcome.

f **Team working** – the ability to work effectively with colleagues towards the accomplishment of a task.

g **Achievement** – although not strictly a skill, evidence of the ability to achieve is an indication of management potential.

h **Networking** – the ability and confidence to seek out named contacts and to use them as a source of personal introduction to further contacts.

There are many more of these skills, and when we look at job analysis you will learn how to seek them out. The most important thing to remember is that you will have to give evidence of situations, work/learning methods, experiences, etc which helped you to develop those skills, so start to think about yourself, what you've done and what you've got to offer *now*!

 Activity 1.2

Let's take two of these skills and see if you can start to think of evidence. Team working is a popular one with employers – it is rare that you would work totally alone in any job. Write down now what activities or experiences would demonstrate your ability to work as an effective team member.

How did you get on with that? Did it occur to you to include seminars and projects, as well as sport? Did you get a spread of academic and extra-curricular activities? Can you specify what your role was in the team – leader, coordinator, facilitator, scribe, etc?

Now, *problem-solving*. See what you can make of that...

More difficult? That may be because you're interpreting 'problem' in a very narrow way. Think about an employer's requirement and look at the definition again. The emphasis is on your approach – how you face and overcome difficulties and how you develop strategies for coping. For instance, the need to change your project because of unforeseen circumstances, or handling a tricky situation with your landlord – these would be acceptable, it doesn't have to be a major disaster that you recall.

Let's try this out on an application form question. Look at that second one again and see if you can draft an answer, using some of the skills vocabulary.

'What have been the most important events in your life so far? Explain what happened and why they are of significance.'

How was that? Read it through from the employer's point of view. What does it say about you? Is it a purely narrative account with facts and figures? If so, you're missing a great opportunity. Or does it *evaluate* the events – giving reasons for their significance in terms of your personal development or subsequent actions? Does it give clues about your ability to deal with situations and your response to challenge? If not, have another attempt.

What about this one?

'List two or three words which a friend may use to describe you. Can you give examples of actual situations which would have merited this description?'

Well done! You're getting the hang of this now, aren't you?

Job analysis

Knowing what you've got to offer is all well and good, but you also need to take into account the other side of the equation – what does the job require?

With most advertised jobs you get some form of job description. This can vary from a glossy brochure with lots of profiles of young graduates to a paragraph in a newspaper. Whatever details you have, make the most of them, by analysing the content. Selectors want the best people, so it's in their interest to give enough information to attract the best people. Sometimes it's easy to find out all you want to know, but sometimes you need to read between the lines.

Let's take an example. This excerpt from the graduate brochure of a leading retailer is explicit:

> *'Drive and determination, plus resilience and stamina are the basic requirements needed to succeed on this scheme. As you will be running your own department after only six months, you will also need to demonstrate strong leadership qualities and excellent interpersonal skills.'*

No excuse, here, for failing to target your application. Obviously you need to give evidence of the ownership of these skills and also to find more explicit detail about the tasks of the job – but that's usually available in the brochure.

Another example, this time for marketing with an international consumer goods business:

> *'What we look for in you: intellectual rigour, analytical ability, commitment, determination, enthusiasm, debating skills and flexibility.'*

Rather a tall order – but at least you're prepared. So when you're filling in this company's application form and they ask you about suitability for the job, or about achievements, you can refer to their list of qualities and make your response accordingly.

If you're saying to yourself – 'That's easy. With that sort of list I can use the words and make my statements fit in with what they want, even if I haven't got all the qualities' – *beware*. Recruitment is a two-way process – the recruiter wants the right person and you want a job – but *the right job*. So be honest with yourself when you're reading these job descriptions. Is it really for you? Will you be able to meet those expectations? Will you want to work for a company which has those expectations? If you are doubtful, get more information or talk to a careers adviser. If the answer is no, then forget it, you'll only have to go through all this again next year, when you eventually realise your mistake and leave.

Sometimes you don't get the full picture from a job description and you have to work harder to draw out the qualities. Let's look at the profile approach favoured by some recruiters.

'I'm now with Our Price Videos in London, which is very different from

WH Smith Retail. It's a small but rapidly growing business. There are very few ground rules and almost no hierarchy – it was the MD who taught me to use the computer!

'Communication is very important in this job. I need to know what is happening in the video business. I talk to the buyers, but I've also developed my own contacts with the video suppliers who I speak to practically every day. If there is a new title or range to promote I discuss with the suppliers how we are going to do it and agree a charge. I then have to brief a design agency on exactly what we want for the advertising display. They can come back to me with some rough designs from which I select one.

'Decisions have to be made quickly in this business and because it's so small and new you have to be a real entrepreneur, prepared to do everything yourself. I wouldn't recommend it to everyone, but it certainly suits me.'

 ## Activity 1.3

Write down the skills/personal qualities required of this last job.

Reading between the lines, are there other things you can say?

I hope that this has given you an insight into the importance of reading job descriptions with an attentive eye. Don't miss the implied qualities, or the suggested ethos of a company. It may make all the difference to your application.

 ## Activity 1.3 – solution

Here's my list. Compare it with your own.

    a Communication skills – oral and written.
    b Team work and the ability to mix at all levels.
    c Networking.
    d Liaison skills.
    e Taking initiative and working independently.
    f Planning and organisation.
    g Decision making including sound judgement.
    h Entrepreneurial skills (encompasses many of the above).
    i Flexibility.
    j Rapid assimilation of information.

And implied by the style and words of the profile:

   k Commitment (probably involves irregular hours).
   l Outgoing personality.
   m Capacity to thrive on pressure.
   n Interest in product, not just the job.

You may very well have got different qualities or a longer list – whatever you managed to glean, well done – this is an important stage in tailoring your application. You can apply this method to any job description, short or long, and come up with extra information to give you an edge over the other applicants.

Before we go on to look at the process of writing applications, let me restate the importance of the exercises you've just done.

Looking at yourself and looking at the job are essential before you put pen to paper.

 Activity 1.4

Summarise what you've learned from these exercises.

 Activity 1.5

Now note down any further action you need to take, eg look at self-assessment material at the CAS, or use *Prospect* (see Chapter 4, Bibliography).

We are now going to move on to the practicalities of written applications, starting with the *curriculum vitae*. So maybe now is a good time to have a break and return refreshed and ready for the fray!

2 The curriculum vitae

The term 'curriculum vitae' means 'the course of life', but this should obviously not be taken too literally. Employers are generally not interested in events before the age of 16 unless you were in the child prodigy league! Rather you should look at a CV as a reflection of your adult educational and work career and, by implication, a dynamic device. I know what you're thinking, *'Yes, that's me – dynamic!'*, but actually I mean dynamic in the sense of moving/changing/developing, not static. This may be the first CV you've ever written, but it won't be the last. You won't be able to take it out of your file in five years' time, dust it down and send it for that internal promotion you've just heard about. So, as we look at the basic components and structure of a CV, I'll remind you constantly about updating and reviewing it, so that it always does you justice.

A note, here, about the relationship between the CV and the application form, which differ from one another in purpose and usage. Both are marketing tools and you will be presenting the same kind of information on each, but whereas in your CV you have a great deal of choice over content and presentation, with a form you must work within given parameters and still sell yourself effectively. I deal with the CV first, since you will have to work through some very basic concepts in order to design the best possible CV for you, and this will help you to avoid the pitfall of rushing at an application form without thorough preparation.

The basic sections

 Activity 2.1

I expect you have an idea of what should go into a CV. Note down the sections you would include (just the headings, not the details).

As we go through the main sections, you can check whether you included them in your list and also whether you had additional sections (you'll need to look carefully at the checklist of 'optional extras').

Another thing to bear in mind when you're writing a CV is that you should have a *reason* for everything you include. This is not like an application form, where the selector calls the tune; this is *your* marketing tool: *use it well*.

Personal details

What are you going to include in this? Have a look at these possibilities, consider their relevance and tick one box per entry.

(**1** = Essential; **2** = Not sure how important; **3** = Unnecessary)

	1	2	3
surname	☐	☐	☐
first name	☐	☐	☐
other names	☐	☐	☐
title (eg Mr, Ms, Dr)	☐	☐	☐
marital status	☐	☐	☐
nationality	☐	☐	☐
religion	☐	☐	☐
home address	☐	☐	☐
term address	☐	☐	☐
telephone number	☐	☐	☐
age	☐	☐	☐
date of birth	☐	☐	☐
place of birth	☐	☐	☐
maiden name (if appropriate)	☐	☐	☐
disabilities	☐	☐	☐
driving licence	☐	☐	☐
father's occupation	☐	☐	☐
dependants	☐	☐	☐
geographical mobility	☐	☐	☐

Activity 2.1 – solution

That's quite a list, isn't it? How many of them did you think were essential? The following would be generally regarded as essential:

- surname
- first name
- home and term address
- telephone number
- date of birth (probably).

The rest is optional or, in some cases, irrelevant. If you think that your nationality is important, especially if you are an international student who would need a work permit, then include it. Equally if you would argue with me that marital status, and possibly even dependants, conveys messages of stability, maturity, etc, that's your decision.

Certain things on that list are important but would be better put elsewhere. *Driving licence* is not really a personal detail, and would be better under additional information. Any mention of physical disability needs sensible handling – give it the most appropriate place. Do you need it in personal details, or can you make a positive statement about it elsewhere on the CV? This would be particularly important if you see your 'coping' as an achievement or a difficulty overcome. Then you could incorporate it into details of education, work experience or leisure activities or even under additional information. Are you getting the message?

 Activity 2.2

Certain personal details are essential. List them now.

Other details can be added at your discretion. Always ask yourself why you're adding them and whether they are relevant.

You should now be able to complete the personal details of your CV. Turn to the CV headings on page 31 and do that exercise now. Don't worry about presentation, we'll get to that later.

Education

Selectors are always interested in your education and exam results as an undergraduate or postgraduate, so it's important to present them in the most positive light. Remember that as you progress in your career the detail of your academic courses becomes much less significant as it is overtaken by work experience. However, getting the information together now will save you lots of panicked phone calls home in the future, demanding your O-level/GCSE certificates. So start searching now.

'How far back should I go?'

As a fresh graduate or college leaver, you'll still need to mention O-levels/GCSEs and A-levels, as well as your course. If you're studying on a postgraduate course, you can afford to ignore the O-levels, or at least condense them dramatically. 'What about BTec, how on earth can I condense that list of subjects?' many of you will be saying. The answer is, you can't. Give the main detail in the body of the CV and then, if you feel it's necessary, attach a photocopy of your results certificate.

'What about me – I'm a mature student?'

I agree that it may seem silly to be presenting exams which you took 15–20 years ago, but you probably did some more recent study before coming to university, eg A-levels, Access or OU, and these will compensate for any previous gaps or failures. Remember, also, that vocational qualifications, eg City & Guilds or SRN, should not be overlooked, as they show what you have already achieved. When you're considering what to include in this section, look at it from the selector's point of view – recent events will normally be of greater interest. Your past educational training may be fascinating to you, it may represent your 'roots', but does it need to claim more space, or even as much space as your degree?

'What about my failed A-level Greek?'

How important is the subject to your application? Will the selector be pleased that you have studied the subject even without a pass grade? If so, then include it: 'studied Greek to A-level standard'. Yes, I know – anybody with any sense will know that you failed it! But it's a lot more positive than saying 'A-level Greek grade F'. If the subject is not important, or if you retook it the following year and passed, then don't include the failure.

 ## Activity 2.3

Write down what you will include in the Education section of your CV, and make a note of any questions. Next time you look at the CV headings you'll probably know the answer, but if your query is very individual you may need to consult a tutor or a careers adviser.

 ## Activity 2.4

Before I say anything about work experience, make a list of all the jobs you've done.

Did you include every single one – even the Saturday job in the paper shop when you were 14? Any more?

Now, look at the list with a selector's eye. What is s/he looking for in your record of jobs? Here are a few suggestions:
- relevant experience
- a commitment to holiday work
- evidence of the skills learned
- something to talk about in the interview
- an inkling of 'real life experience'.

Can you think of anything else, especially in your own case? Make a note of it.

Work experience

Most students have to work in their vacations in order to pay off debts and, often, to keep themselves. Very few can find stimulating or relevant jobs, when the only place that's offering work is the local pie factory. But it *is* work (and it may be all you've got to put down) so make the most of it. If I had to choose from my list, I would say that selectors are looking mostly for evidence of skills learned. So what skills did you learn packing pies in the aforementioned factory? Remember what I said earlier about skills – consider personal skills as well as technical/professional skills.

 Activity 2.5

Take any one of your jobs. What did it teach you about yourself, about the work environment? Why would a selector want to know about it? Copy the table below and fill it in. I've given you a starter for free.

Job title	Employer	What did you do?	What did you learn?
Sales assistant	Boots	Served customers, operated till, stacked shelves	Tact, patience, working under pressure, communication skills

Refer back to the earlier section on skills for the key words which tend to crop up in job descriptions. Use them to make the most of your work experience. Don't get carried away though – I have seen examples of excess, eg making a counter job at Pizzaland sound like the managing director of an international company! Have another go with a different job and think hard about what you gained from the job.

Are you beginning to use the right words now? What you have just done is an exercise in analysis. When you are writing your CV you won't have much space, so you will have to condense what you say and cut out any unnecessary detail.

'I've got hundreds of casual jobs, I can't include them all.'

Group casual work together, and give a summary of what you learned generally.

'Some of my work experience is really relevant, but the rest is not. Should I only include the relevant stuff?'

Obviously your relevant work experience will interest an employer particularly, so you need to give it precedence. But if you only include the one relevant job it may look as if you haven't done anything else. Why not split your work experience into two sections: *relevant* and *other*. That way you get the best of both worlds.

'My work experience was so long ago!'

If you're a mature student who's brought up a family you may be presenting jobs you did 15–20 years ago, and then nothing for the last 10 years. This is not really a problem, since selectors accept that mature students (and career changers) are using education as a way of changing direction. You can still note down your previous work and what you learned from it, or you can write a short paragraph about your progress into higher education, including reference to former jobs and your 'time out' with the family and linking it to your present and future plans.

 ## Activity 2.6

Are you ready to fill in this section now? As you're doing it, look always for the positive aspects, but keep it short and concise. Turn to the CV headings on page 31 and do it now.

Let's think about this dynamic CV again. What you've written down for this section reflects the 'newly qualified student' looking for a first permanent job. As I said about the education details, recent events overtake the past and your GCSE/A-levels will gradually fade into insignificance as you accumulate degree and professional qualifications. This is even more true of work experience. In five years' time, when you go for internal promotion, you won't be including your holiday jobs or jobs you did before you came into higher education, you'll be concentrating on your professional experience. So the exercise you've just done has taught you a way of breaking down jobs into tasks, responsibilities and skills, and you will need to do this again and again as you progress through your career.

Activities/interests

 ## Activity 2.7

Why do selectors want to know what you do in your spare time?
Tick which of the following you think are most likely:

a idle curiosity ☐

b something to talk about in the interview ☐

c evidence of personality type ☐

   d to distinguish you from the other 200 geography students
      who have also applied

   e to see the 'whole person'

All are valid reasons, except **a**. If you ticked it, you need to keep this kind of cynicism under control! Perhaps the most dubious reason is **c**, which tends to suggest that selectors are making judgements about you. For example, if you wrote as your interests 'reading, playing patience, listening to music on my personal stereo and solo hill-walking', does this necessarily mean that you are introverted and unable to relate to your peers? Yes, probably it does! So one of the messages must be to give a broad span of interests, *but without inventing any!* You'll be found out!

Another important point about activities/interests is that if you want to say something about yourself, through the things that you like doing, you should give enough information. A list of interests will get the selector yawning in no time, but if you include tantalising detail, s/he may actually want to see you to talk about it. For example, compare the following two examples:

'I enjoy photography and sport, mainly football.'

'I enjoy photography, particularly black and white studies of towns and cities, and I have learned recently to process my own film. My other main interest is sport, mainly football, and I have played for the Hall team this year. This not only keeps me fit, but gives me an opportunity to be part of a team and to mix socially with students from other courses.'

The interests are the same, but the effect is very different.

 ## Activity 2.8

Write down now what you have learned about this student from the second statement.

One more thing before you complete this section. You should be presenting not only what you do for recreation, but also what you do in the student community, eg membership of societies, community action, AIESEC. If you are secretary or a committee member, look at the section on optional extras, but if you are involved in any way it is worth mentioning.

Activity 2.9

So turn to the CV headings on page 31 and do the exercise.

Additional information

You may be wondering what on earth can be left to say! Any thoughts on a few extra things you've got to offer? Look back at the details you've given under the CV headings, and then jot down anything else you think might be important for a selector to know.

Did you include any of the following?
a school prefect
b swimming certificates
c other qualifications, eg typing
d foreign language skills
e driving licence
f computing skills
g treasurer of the Parachute Society.

Certainly **c, d, e,** and **f** are worth including with some detail, eg which language and to what level? use of own car? what computer skills, systems, packages and languages? If you wrote something similar to **a** or **g**, then look at the optional extras section. You may have included other things which haven't occurred to me, so think how important they are, and where you should put them. This may be the place where you want to say something about your health in a positive way. No, I haven't forgotten the swimming certificates. I would merely ask that you consider carefully their relevance to your application.

Referees

It is usual to include the names of referees in a CV, although as you progress through a career this can become awkward. Your first CV as a recently qualified student should include one academic referee – probably course leader or a tutor who knows you well – and, if possible, a work-related referee. This may be relatively straightforward if you have done a placement as part of your course, but if not you can use a vacation employer. Should you feel that this is not appropriate for some reason, you can use a second academic referee or someone who has known you for a long time – not a relative though.

Remember to ask permission. Most academic tutors complete references for students all the time, but you may need to check that they know your career interests.

For other referees, it is useful to give them a copy of your CV, just to remind them who you are!

 Activity 2.10

Turn to the CV headings (page 31) and make a note of possible referees. It is always useful to have at least three to choose from, in case of the absence of any one of them.

Optional extras

a   Positions of responsibility
Some companies are keen to see evidence of leadership skills, so it's often worth including your committee or society jobs, back to 6th form at school. If you have lots, such as team captain for several sports, county standard, Student Union posts, you need a separate section. If, on the other hand, you have only one or two, or none at all, don't worry – not everyone has the chance or the desire to be captain of everything from the age of 5. You simply include what you've done in your activities/interests section.

b   Awards/scholarships/exhibitions
If the above applies to you, you should be proud of it – after all it's an achievement. For some students, for example, of visual/performing arts, it is crucial to include details of awards and exhibitions, and you would certainly need to create a special place in your CV for this. For other students it may be just the one award, eg science prize at school or best student award at university. Again, you can include it under additional information, but if you want to highlight it, then let it stand alone.

c   Personal statement
For some people this is cringe time as it smacks of self-publicity. In fact, it can be very effective to make a statement about yourself and your aspirations in a CV. It doesn't have to be over-the-top or brash – it's better to make it precise and clear, so that a selector knows exactly what you want and what you feel you have to offer. Think about it. You'll find an example on page 29. If it appeals to you, then try drafting your own. If you're still not tempted, then that's OK.

I've outlined three areas of optional extras, but there may be others which are appropriate for you. As I keep saying, this CV is yours – you can add other sections as you wish, so long as you bear in mind the basic guidelines about length and clarity.

Activity 2.11

So, if you have optional extras to add, then complete the section in the CV headings on page 31 now.

Congratulations! You've got the material ready – that's half the battle. Now you've got to put it together.

Putting your CV together

You know you've got a lot to offer – just look at all the information needed on a CV! But information needs organising and presenting in the most effective way. Different people have different opinions about CVs. Many books will show you an example of a one page CV, and others will prefer glossy folders with coloured paper and even photos. Oh no, not the mug shot!

 Activity 2.12

A short quiz about CVs. Answer true or false to the following.

		T	**F**
a	A CV should be short (one side of A4)	☐	☐
b	There is only one way of doing a CV	☐	☐
c	You should attach a recent photograph	☐	☐
d	You don't need a CV for most graduate jobs	☐	☐
e	An agency gives you the most professional CV	☐	☐

So you have some opinions about how a CV ought to be presented. Let's think about this from your point of view. You know what a CV is and what goes into it, and I hope that you've remembered that the main difference between an application form and a CV is that with a CV you're not forced to answer certain questions or give certain information in a certain order. You choose what goes into your CV and so you can also choose what goes where. This frees you from the dreadful 'ought' of the first sentence. Yes, there are guidelines, but no hard and fast rules – you can be as creative or as traditional as you want.

So if we look at your assumptions, based on the 'true and false' quiz, the only statement which is true is **a**, and then only up to the brackets. There's short and there's short. One side of A4 will not be enough for most people, but selectors have limited time and if you present a five-page document – beautiful though it might be – it will be seen, at this stage of your career, as excessive. Aim for two sides of A4 and you won't go far wrong.

Let me say something about statement **d**. It is true that large graduate recruiters have their own application forms, and even medium-sized firms may ask for a standard application form, so you are unlikely to use a CV for 'milkround' companies. However, you may see vacancies at any time of the year, in journals, vacancy lists and the press, which require a CV, and there is nothing worse than having to throw a CV together overnight. Prepare your CV in plenty of time and, if possible, keep it on disk so that you can update it regularly.

A word about *agencies*. You may feel that it is worth spending a considerable amount of money on a CV service, since you assume that an agency must know how to do it better than you. Not necessarily! Agencies will have a standard package for presentation which may not be the way you want your CV to look. There is absolutely no need to use an agency at this stage in your career: selectors don't expect it, they want clear, interesting information which looks good and is easy to read. Totally within your limits – you and the word processor, that is! As you progress in your career you may feel that a professionally produced CV is a wise investment, particularly in certain sectors of business, but by then the expectations of selectors will be different and, more importantly, you'll have more money.

You're now ready to write your CV. I don't want to give you just one example of a 'good' CV, as you might just copy the format without thinking about your particular needs. So I'm going to give you several examples, to illustrate how flexible you can be.

Curriculum Vitae

Elizabeth Walterton

25 Vicarage Close, Barnsley, South Yorkshire

Date of birth: 16.4.73   Nationality: British

Education/qualifications

St Mary's Comprehensive	GCSE English	A
Barnsley	Maths	C
1984–90	French	B
	German	B
	Biology	B
	History	A
	Geography	C
	Home economics	C
Barnsley College of		
Further Education	A-level English	B
1990–93	History	C
	German	C
South Yorkshire University		
1993–96	BA(Hons) Combined Arts	

Work experience

1987–90	Woolworths	Saturday sales assistant
1993	WH Smith	Summer holiday work in shop
1994	Watersports Ltd	Summer job – office and shop
1995	Watersports Ltd	Summer job – office

Activities and interests

Windsurfing, water-skiing, reading, dancing and Pop-mobility

Additional information

Clean driving licence. Word-processing. French and German

Referees

Dr S. Martin   Mr J. Torr
Dept of English Studies   Watersports Ltd
South Yorkshire University   Arndale Centre
Rotherham R23 4XD   Barnsley B7 2IK

This CV contains all the important sections and is short and neatly presented. But what do you actually find out about this applicant?

 Activity 2.13

Can you write down five things about this person from her CV?

Well done if you managed five. I bet they were all facts, such as where she lives, what she's studying. Did you manage to form any impression of her? Is she sociable (she goes windsurfing – usually you do that in a club)? Has she got any skills to sell (surely you learn something from all that work)? What's she doing in her course? (Combined Arts is a bit vague, isn't it?)

 Activity 2.14

Which sections of Elizabeth's CV could she expand to let some personal details show through? Which parts would you expand?

The next two pages give an alternative of Elizabeth's CV. The facts are the same but the emphasis is different and the detail is increased.

Curriculum Vitae

Elizabeth Walterton

25 Vicarage Close	16 Commonwealth Road
Barnsley	Rotherham
South Yorkshire	South Yorkshire
(Home Address)	(Term Address)
01226 5186741	01709 6623459

Date of birth: 16.4.73

Education/qualifications

BA (Hons) Combined Arts	South Yorkshire University
	1993–96

Main subjects:
Year 1: English, German and Sociology
Year 2: English, German and Philosophy
Year 3: English, Philosophy and Modern German Literature

21

Subsidiaries:
Information Technology and Linguistics

During my second year I attended a German university for four weeks and attended language and culture classes with German students.
My final year dissertation is on the subject of English theatre in the late 19th century.

A-levels:	English	B	Barnsley College of Further Education
	History	C	1993
	German	C	

GCSEs:	8 subjects	St Mary's Comprehensive School
	(incl. Maths)	Barnsley 1989

Work experience

Watersports Ltd, Barnsley 1994–95

I worked for this company for two summer vacations. It is a small retail and hire shop, supplying watersports equipment to clubs and individuals. Because I am a keen windsurfer and water skier I was able to help advise customers and I thoroughly enjoyed this contact with the public. As I became more familiar with the hire system I was often given the responsibility for contacting clients and suppliers and filling in the paperwork. In my second vacation, the owner left me solely in charge of the office, which was an excellent way of learning how a small business runs – hectic but very satisfying! I found my knowledge of computing very valuable.

WH Smith 1993

This was a small branch of Smiths, which meant that we did not have to deal with the same range of products as a high street branch. However, it did give me the chance to do everything in the shop, from serving to making up the paper bills. I enjoyed the real feeling of working in a team, which I had not experienced before.

Woolworths 1987–90

I had a Saturday job in Woolworths while I was at school, and although I found the job rather routine – filling shelves all day – it was my first experience of work and made me much more confident when talking to people.

Activities/interests

I have been interested in water sports since school, particularly windsurfing and water-skiing. My local leisure centre in Barnsley organised courses and I joined a local club. Windsurfing is a very sociable sport, as well as being very demanding in terms of fitness. You quickly learn to help one another and you certainly learn perseverance and a sense of humour. I have continued this sport at university, and I am secretary of the Windsurfing Club this year.

My other interests include reading (particularly fantasy novels), dancing and Pop-mobility, which helps my general level of fitness.

Additional information

I hold a clean driving licence and hope to buy my own car at the end of this year.

As part of my course I have studied Information Technology, which has included some basic programming skills and also word-processing. I am familiar, particularly, with Word Perfect.

My German is fluent and I can converse quite easily in French.

Referees

Dr S. Martin
Dept of English Studies
South Yorkshire University
Rotherham R23 4XD

Mr J. Torr
Watersports Ltd
Arndale Centre
Barnsley B7 2IK

You can see from this second example that Elizabeth has given more details about what she considers would be important (her degree course and her work experience) and less about her GCSE exams. If you look at her section Activities/interests you will find much more about herself – details of commitment, personal qualities, responsibilities, etc. Not just a list – more a list with a purpose!

So it's very important to look at the information you have under the CV headings, and decide what is important and what you can use to 'sell' your skills and qualities.

Why not try a *skills profile approach*? Instead of using the traditional format of sections, you could set out your experience in terms of the skills required for the job, linking your evidence in with each skill.

The advantage of this approach is that you can use key words which are important to the selector and which make an early positive impact. But beware of waffling! If you use a skills profile, then make sure that you give concrete evidence, not just vague generalisation.

You can see the effect of this approach in the next example of a CV. Again, the choice is yours. If you feel more comfortable with a straightforward format, then put your CV together like that. I'm trying to make you see that you can be flexible if you choose.

Activity 2.15

When you have looked at the next example, I want you to write your own CV, using all the information you have gathered. Think about the content, the presentation and whether it will be appropriate for the employers you will be approaching.

Over to you!

Curriculum Vitae

Elizabeth Walterton

25 Vicarage Close	16 Commonwealth Road
Barnsley	Rotherham
South Yorkshire	South Yorkshire
(Home Address)	(Term Address)
01226 5186741	01709 6623459

Date of birth: 16.4.73

Education/qualifications

BA (Hons) Combined Arts   South Yorkshire University
                                       1993–96

Main subjects:
Year 1: English, German and Sociology
Year 2: English, German and Philosophy
Year 3: English, Philosophy and Modern German Literature

Subsidiaries:
Information Technology and Linguistics

During my second year I attended a German university for four weeks and attended language and culture classes with German students.
My final year dissertation is on the subject of English theatre in the late 19th century.

A-levels:	English	B	Barnsley College of Further Education
	History	C	1993
	German	C	

| GCSEs: | 8 subjects (incl. Maths) | St Mary's Comprehensive School Barnsley 1990 |

Skills/personal qualities

a Persuasiveness

I have been involved in many different aspects of sales work, and in my most recent job at Watersports Ltd I was dealing with knowledgeable customers who were very demanding in their requirements.

b Initiative

I enjoy making decisions and working on my own initiative. My employer at Watersports Ltd was happy to leave me to run the office on my own and I rose to the challenge of this, often having to place orders for equipment in his absence.

c Communication skills

I have always achieved high grades in my written assignments at university and have also had the chance to give presentations on course work. Again, my sales experience has given me great confidence in dealing tactfully with the general public.

d Commitment

My motivation and commitment can be seen in my long-standing interest in windsurfing, which has made demands of time and perseverance over the years. I have trained hard to achieve a good technique and I have also undertaken to be an active member of the University Club this year. I feel that I bring this level of commitment to work and leisure.

e Team working

Both on my course and in my work and leisure activity, I try to be an active team member. In course projects I find this is the ideal way to work, by learning from one another, and my vacation jobs have taught me to mix with people from very varied backgrounds.

Work experience

Watersports Ltd, Barnsley 1994–95

I worked for this company for two summer vacations. It is a small retail and hire shop, supplying watersports equipment to clubs and individuals. At first I worked in the shop, but in my second summer my boss left me in charge of the office – which was a wonderful insight into the running of a small business.

WH Smith 1993

This was a small branch of Smiths, which meant that we worked as a close team, dealing with everything from sales to the paper bills.

Woolworths 1987–90

This was my Saturday job, while I was at school, and although it was fairly routine work, it was an introduction to retailing.

Additional information
- Clean driving licence
- Basic programming skills and extensive use of Word Perfect
- Fluent German and conversational French

Referees

Dr S. Martin (Academic)
Dept of English Studies
South Yorkshire University
Rotherham R23 4XD

Mr J. Torr (Work related)
Watersports Ltd
Arndale Centre
Barnsley B7 2IK

When to use a CV

As I said in the previous section, there will be occasions when a CV is not required, such as graduate recruitment in the Autumn and Spring terms, which is virtually all by application form. But you can be asked for a CV for differing purposes: for holiday work, for a postgraduate course, for working overseas, as well as for responding to vacancies which specify one.

So, you will use a CV *in response* to an advertised opportunity. You will also use a CV if you approach companies or organisations *speculatively*. In other words, if you are interested in a company/organisation, but you haven't seen any advertised vacancies, you can write to ask them to consider you for any future positions. You can also use this approach if you're looking for work experience.

Normally, you should not include a CV with an application form, unless invited to do so. The reason for this is that most selectors consider their application form adequate, and therefore a CV is simply duplication and extra bits of paper. If you truly feel that a particular application form does not allow you the opportunity to sell yourself, because of lack of space or appropriate questions, then you can decide to send a CV to accompany it – but consider well, you can end up irritating selectors *by not following instructions*.

The covering letter

A CV requires a covering letter. It is through this letter that you *personalise* your approach to an employer. If you don't do this it will look as though you are sending a standard CV to a list of companies without any real thought.

Not only does a letter add a personal touch, but it gives you *another chance to sell yourself*. By summarising the most relevant aspects of your experience, and by highlighting your suitability for the job, you tempt the selector into looking more closely at your details. Which is what it's all about, isn't it?

Let's look at the main paragraphs you should include in a covering letter.

a What you're applying for and where you saw it advertised. Also indicate your present situation.
b Draw attention to relevant aspects of your experience: academic and work. Say what you learned and how it would be useful to the selector.
c Sell yourself on the basis of your skills and personal qualities, making sure that these match up with the requirements of the job.
d Say something about the company/organisation – what attracts you to apply to them and what you know about them (*subtle* flattery, please!).
e Close with some reference to availability for interview and the usual signing-off phrases.

If your approach to an employer is *speculative*, then the same messages apply, except that, of course, your opening paragraph would state quite clearly why you are writing.

Keep your letter relatively brief; probably one side of A4, though this is only a guideline. If you do find yourself getting to the bottom of the second page, I suggest you read it through and decide what's really important; selectors have only limited time. *Make it clear, concise and interesting.*

You can handwrite a covering letter. Many selectors like to see your script; but, equally, if your handwriting is appalling or if you feel you need to create a business style, then it is acceptable to type it.

Here is an example of a covering letter to accompany a CV in response to an advertisement for a graduate trainee in accountancy.

24 Manor Road
Littlebridge
Kent

24.5.96

Mr P. Cotingham
Pockitt & Jingle
Main St
Fossington
Hants.

Dear Mr Cotingham,

I am writing in response to your advertisement for a trainee accountant, included in the Current Vacancy list from Littlebridge University where I am in the final year of an Economics degree.

As you will see from my CV, I took a year out between A-levels and university to work in a local accountancy firm. Although the work was initially clerical, I soon progressed to audit and thoroughly enjoyed this. In fact, it was this experience, together with my success at A-level Economics, which determined my choice of degree subject.

During my studies at Littlebridge University, I have opted for modules relating to accounting and business economics, and have achieved good results in these. My previous work experience has enabled me to find summer placements in accountancy firms, and I now look forward to entering the profession full time.

Your firm is of particular interest to me because it is of medium size and will, therefore, allow me to become involved quickly as a team member. I enjoy challenges and have always found problem-solving very satisfying. For these reasons the accountancy profession appears to suit my personality and skills and I am now fully committed to this career. I am also keen to progress rapidly towards a professional qualification and I notice that you place great emphasis on training.

I look forward to the opportunity to discuss my experience with you at interview. My final exams fall in the two weeks of 9th to 23rd June.

Yours sincerely,

John Chambers

Moving on

Let's look at how your CV will change as you move from job to job.

 Activity 2.16

Think about yourself in three year's time. Where do you hope to be? How will your CV reflect this? Look at the checklist below and tick the statements you agree with.

a   I will still need to include GCSE/A-levels ☐

b   I will still need to give a description of my final year project ☐

c   My work experience will reflect recent positions not vacation work ☐

d   I will still need an academic referee ☐

e   Basically I can simply add on to my present CV extra information about my job ☐

f   I won't have changed that much in three years ☐

Did you feel confident about your answers to these questions? Thinking ahead is difficult, especially when you don't know what you'll be doing in a few months' time, never mind three years. Simply remember that your CV is a dynamic tool – it has to change with you.

As you move from your first graduate position into 'middle management' or the equivalent you need to show a selector what you've achieved and how you've developed through that first job, so that s/he can judge your potential. So, in most cases, the only statement in that list which is true is **c**. If you ticked any more, then think why and after you've looked at the next example, you may want to change your opinion.

Let's look at Elizabeth's CV three years on, as she approaches promotion.

Curriculum Vitae: Elizabeth Walterton

Personal statement
I have a thorough grounding in sales administration and I am now ready to take on a managerial function, which would build on my existing knowledge and skills and would enable me to make a positive contribution to the future of the company.

Present position: Sales Administrator

Responsibilities:
- processing of orders/accounts
- preparation of sales figures for management meetings
- liaison with sales team and customers
- liaison with internal departments, primarily Marketing and Production
- supervision of clerical/administrative staff
- preparation of export documentation.

Skills/personal qualities
- excellent organisational ability
- effective team working
- good communication skills, both written and oral
- tact and diplomacy – particularly important in 'delicate' internal negotiations
- persuasiveness
- high level of adaptability and an acceptance that sales is not a 9–5 job!
- problem-solving
- commitment and a professional approach to my job.

Previous position: Graduate Trainee (Sales)

During this two-year training programme I was given an overview of the sales function, initially through projects, but then through placements in Marketing,

---

Finance and Production. I even spent time 'on the road' with the sales representatives – an experience which proved very useful when I eventually had to manage my own team. At the end of my training period I chose to work in sales administration, as this position seemed ideal for my particular skills and also fitted in with my long-term ambition to become a National Accounts Manager.

Training courses

Time management	1996
Personal effectiveness	1996
Managing a team	1997
Outward Bound experience	1997

All these courses were undertaken as part of my graduate programme.

ISMM/City and Guilds Sales Management – part-time course Southampton Technical College 1996 – completion in 1998.

Activities/interests

I have maintained an interest in watersports since my school years, especially windsurfing. While at university I was an active member of the Windsurfing Club and found the activity both physically demanding and extremely enjoyable. I have been fortunate enough to be able to continue this sport in Southampton by joining a local club and this activity occupies most of my spare time. Whenever possible, I go to the theatre and cinema, although my part-time study takes up much of my available free time, especially around exams!

Education

BA (Hons) Combined Arts 2:i   South Yorkshire University 1993–96

Main subjects: English and German, with subsidiary Sociology
Optional courses in Information Technology and Linguistics

During my second year I attended a German university for four weeks.

A-levels – English (B) History (C) German (C)
GCSE – 8 subjects (incl. Maths)

Additional information

I hold a clean driving licence and own my own car. In the course of my work in sales administration I have used a computer extensively for analysis of data and production of charts, graphs, tables, etc.

My German is still fluent, and I can converse easily in French.

Personal details

29 Harbour View
Southampton
SO6 8PN
Telephone: 01703 765987

Date of birth: 16.4.73

Curriculum vitae exercise

Personal details

_____
_____

Education

_____
_____

Work experience

_____
_____

Activities/interests

_____
_____

Additional information

_____
_____

Referees

_____
_____

Optional extras

_____
_____

Personal statement

_____
_____

3 The application form

If you have already completed the section on the curriculum vitae you will be familiar with the idea of 'marketing' yourself on paper, but for many graduate positions, you will have to use an application form. I drew your attention, in Chapter 1, to the type of questions which are currently appearing on these instruments of torture, so you are bright enough to realise that filling in forms is time consuming. Gone are the days when you could knock off ten applications in the course of an evening and still have time to down your usual quota of pints in the local hostelry! It's now quite common to expect to spend several hours (if not days) on each form.

The questions are demanding, there's usually a blank page for your personal statement, and competition for jobs is so stiff that you must do the whole thing well.

I also wrote in Chapter 1 about the need for self-assessment and job analysis (pages 2–3 and 5–7), especially when you're asked to evaluate experiences, but there are equally important messages about the presentation of the form. Let's run through these:

a Follow the instructions on the form.
b Read the whole form through first before putting pen to paper.
c Either photocopy the form or do a draft first, in order to see how your answers will fit the available space.
d Use black ink.
e If you use additional sheets, make sure you put your name on them and attach them securely.
f Choose the right size envelope – it's OK to fold a form neatly, but *not too much* (concertinas are difficult to read).
g Photocopy your completed form ready for interview revision.
h Include a short covering letter.

A standard application form

Standard application forms (SAFs) are available from your Careers Service, and some employers use these instead of devising their own. Do a practice run using one of these. It will be a very good introduction to form filling and will also force you to collect your 'data' together. Once you've filled in an SAF you are ready to tackle the more demanding forms and, if you've chosen to do this section of the book first, you can use the information when you come to write a CV.

Are you sitting comfortably? Then I'll begin. Throughout this chapter I will refer to comments already made about CV preparation. This will save irritating repetition if you've completed that chapter and equally, if you haven't, you will be able to 'plug in' to the appropriate messages.

Page 1

Page 1 the factual information required on most application forms. Note the instructions at the top of the form and also the specific demands of each section. You should not have any problems completing this page, other than remembering dates! As I mentioned in the previous chapter, you have very little scope for choice on a form, unlike the CV. Some students feel that their educational history does not fit easily into the available space, eg BTec results/mature students. I have made comments about this in Education, on page 11.

 Activity 3.1

Now fill in the first page of your form, referring to the CV headings on page 31 if appropriate.

Page 2

On this page usually you are asked to evaluate your experiences in three areas – academic work, employment and leisure activities. Note the word evaluate – this is not purely factual. You are trying to give evidence of the skills you possess so that a selector can see that you have what s/he wants. Refer to my comments in Self-assessment, on page 2, and in Skills and personal qualities, page 3.

Every application form will cover these areas in one way or another, so it is a good idea to sort out now what you are going to say about the benefits of work and leisure activities. However, heed a word of warning. You should not go for a model answer – there is a difference here between the use of the CV and the form. Your CV will be standard, and the covering letter will personalise the approach, but with a form you must reflect the particular needs of the employer in your answers. For example, suppose you are asked to

> *'Describe any aspect of your course of particular interest to you and/or of relevance to your application.'*

Let's assume that you have two major things to sell here: an academic project, which has some relevance to your intended career, and a subsidiary in business statistics. Both are important, but you may decide, from what you've read in the graduate brochure, that one employer will be particularly impressed with relevant experience, whereas another may appreciate the business skills you've learned. So you vary the order and the emphasis.

I hope that this makes it clear how unwise it is to duplicate application forms to different employers. There will always be different needs and different emphases which you need to reflect in your answers.

In summary: facts alone will not do. You know, from your job analysis, what the employer is looking for. You know, from your self-assessment, what you have to offer. Put the two together, and make your answer interesting and appropriate.

 Activity 3.2

Now fill in the questions on page 2 of your form, referring to your notes under the CV headings on page 31.

Page 3

Here we have what might be termed the 'crunch' question – *why do you want the job and why should we appoint you?* This is where the marketing becomes explicit and any natural reserve has to take a back seat. You want this job, don't you? (If you don't, then you have a strange way of passing the time!) So you have to tell the selector why and then give enough 'evidence of suitability', ie personal skills, experience, job knowledge, and so on, to get an interview.

 Activity 3.3

Make a first draft now, using a job you're considering.

> *'Explain what attracts you about the type(s) of work for which you are applying and offer evidence of your suitability.'*

Now look at my checklist and tick off what you achieved.

a Did you think about the requirements of the job before you put pen to paper (in a real situation this would mean re-reading brochures, job descriptions, etc)?

b Did you describe the origins of your interest, eg arising out of the course/work experience/leisure activity, and plot its progress?

c Did you mention action taken, eg the pursuit of relevant work experience, voluntary work, attendance at presentations?

d Did you mention aspects of the job/training specifically? This shows that you know something about it.

e Did you then link what you know to what you have to offer – academic/technical skills (if appropriate), experience and personal qualities?

f Did you say positive things about yourself, using your 'skills vocabulary'?

g Did you mention some aspect of the company/organisation specifically, so that it didn't look as if you wrote the same thing on every form?

h Does it impress you when you read it through or does it make you cringe? (You may have to come to terms with the 'cringe factor'.)

If you ticked a fair number of these questions, then you're on the right lines. Remember this is not a comprehensive list, but just a few prompts to bear in mind when you read it again. Many forms will allow you a whole page for this statement *and* will invite you to attach additional sheets, so it has to be tackled thoroughly.

The remainder of page 3 is generally a mix of questions on various aspects of administrative importance, eg health, mobility. Two are particularly significant: the question of points for interview and the additional information item. The former is probably just an aide for the future interviewer, so s/he can prepare any specific facts, but it also gives an indication of your interest in the company and the job. Equally, the latter is an opportunity to present information which does not fit into other questions, but will interest the selector and may gain you extra points.

I have discussed choice of referees on page 16, so you can refer to this if necessary before completing this page of the form.

Have you noticed where you must sign and date the form? Failing to do this can lead to automatic binning!

 Activity 3.4

Now turn to your SAF and complete page 3, re-drafting your answer to the 'crunch' question, if necessary.

Page 4 of the SAF is for monitoring purposes and will not appear on every employer form.

Once you've completed this exercise, you will be able to keep this form as a good reference for any other you complete.

I do not intend to instruct you in how to complete individual application form questions. If you have read and understood the sections on self-assessment and job analysis you should be ready to tackle anything thrown at you. Simply remember that the function of an application form is to *inform* and *interest* the selector. You must regard it as a marketing tool, so include details of *suitability, skills, personal qualities* and let your *personality* show through. Impress the selector with your knowledge of the job/course and *be positive – distinguish yourself.* That's the way to get an interview. Objective achieved!

The covering letter

A note about letters with application forms. These do not really need to be the full covering letter described in When to use a CV on page 26. In fact, you may find that any extra bits of paper are detached by a secretary. However forms do merit a short accompanying letter, indicating the position applied for and the source of the vacancy. You can also use the letter to point out any unusual features of your application, eg that the company is not visiting your institution or the implications of semester dates for interviews. An example is given next.

---

13 Green Road
Barnsley
BS2 8TR

12.5.96

Ms S. Tempest
Blake's Emporium
Chattel Road
Leeds
LS5 9YO

Dear Ms Tempest

I enclose my application form for the Trainee Manager vacancy, as advertised in Blankfield University Current Vacancies.

As stated on my form, I am in the final year of a degree course in Emporium Management and will be available for interviews at any time except from 9th to 23rd June, when I have my exams.

I look forward to hearing from you in due course.

Yours sincerely,

John Mason

---

4 Bibliography

Self-assessment

Bolles, R. N. (1990) *What colour is your parachute?*, California, Ten Speed Press. A practical manual.

Hoopson, B. and Scally, M. (1991) *Build your own rainbow*, Lifeskills Associates. Very user-friendly.

Careers Advisory Service resources

Your Careers Advisory Service holds a great deal of information about self-assessment and job-hunting, much of which is produced by AGCAS (The Association of Graduate Careers Advisory Services). The following material is particularly relevant:

Where next? Exploring your future. A practical career-planning workbook.

Applications and interviews. A very useful booklet containing hints about CVs and application forms.

Write giving full details. A 20-minute video on written applications.

Many university careers services have a computer program, *Prospect*, which serves as an aid to self-assessment and career choice.

Part B: Being interviewed

Introduction

This part aims to provide an introduction to the basics of interview preparation and performance, to enable students to make the most of this opportunity for self-marketing.

If you have limited experience of interviews, or if that experience has been negative so far, don't worry – your performance can be improved through a greater understanding of technique and presentation.

Objectives

At the end of the exercises in Part B you should be able to:
- understand the purpose of the selection interview and be familiar with two different models;
- prepare for standard areas of questioning and predict specific questions by analysing an application form;
- develop a strategy for the unstructured interview;
- analyse your own competence in verbal and non-verbal interview behaviour and design an action plan for future improvement.

This book is designed to enable you to work at your own pace and select the chapters or activities most appropriate for you at any given time.

In this part you will be presented with information about interview preparation and procedure and then questioned to check your understanding. You will perform exercises as you go through the text and these will form the basis of your preparation for any interview which you may attend in the future.

Take the challenge!

5 What is an interview?

Silly question? Everyone has an idea of what to expect from an interview – usually a battery of questions. But what is the purpose of an interview? Silly question again! Obviously the purpose of a selection interview is to select someone! But how does the interview achieve that? Asking questions and getting answers will not alone allow the interviewer to make a decision. It is the interpretation of the answers which counts and, perhaps more importantly, the communication which develops between interviewer and interviewee.

So, it's not an interrogation. Nor is it a kind of victimisation. The ideal of the interview is two-way communication. Unless you are encouraged to talk, and unless you take the opportunity to talk, the interviewer will learn very little about you and will not be able to decide about your suitability for the job.

Perhaps this is the point at which to allow you to grumble about all those awful interviews you've had where two-way communication certainly didn't happen and you came out wondering what had hit you!

 Activity 5.1

Think about those occasions and make a note of why the experience was not a good one.

Now look at your comments. What went wrong? It will normally be one of two things:

a you were not well-enough prepared;
b the interviewer was not competent.

You have to be very honest here – it's always easier to say *'the questions were stupid'* than to admit that you couldn't answer them. Putting the blame on the interviewer may make you feel better, but you won't learn anything from the experience.

This part is about performing well at interviews and much of that is to do with preparation – so we can deal with any problems in that area. However, what you can't control is the behaviour of the interviewer. Some are just not very good or haven't been trained. This may make the experience very frustrating for you, but it does not negate the need for preparation. You should approach every interview expecting the highest level of 'good practice' and, if it turns out differently, then at least you can attempt to take some control of the proceedings. More of that later.

So start being positive. Put all the bad experiences behind you and see how you can make the most of the 'next time'.

Styles of interviewing

The majority of people involved in recruitment are trained in selection interviewing. They will not all be trained in the same way. Individual companies design their own application forms and their own interview assessment models. You will not know what these models are, but I can introduce you to one very common type – that of the behavioural interview.

Now, settle down, this is not going to be a psychology lecture. It will take only a few lines, but they may be the most important few lines you will read for a while!

What is behavioural interviewing? It is, quite simply, getting a candidate to describe events in the past (or sometimes the present) which can be used to predict whether the individual will, in the future, demonstrate skills which are important for a specific job. Just as on application forms you are asked to describe achievements in terms of 'when you did it', 'how you did it', 'what the results were' etc, so similar questions will crop up in the interview, eg:

> *'Give me an example of a time when you were able to persuade someone of your point of view.'*

> *'When you had to do a piece of work in college which was really uninteresting to you, how did you deal with it?'*

Can you see the connections? By looking at your past achievements and at the way you have handled situations, selectors judge how well you will cope with particular aspects of a job in the future.

In terms of your preparation for the interview the message is clear. You should give concrete evidence to support your statements – general comments like *'I'm good at talking to people'* are not enough; you will receive the challenge *'Give me an example.'*

Not all interviewers will use a behavioural model – some will have a fixed assessment schedule, as described in the next section. However, all selectors will appreciate specific information rather than generalisms, so preparing for this model will ensure that you have covered the ground thoroughly.

Now that you can see, in theory, what the interview is all about, let's consider your practical preparation. In order to prepare well, you must look at it from both sides: the interviewer and yourself.

What do you think an employer wants from the interview?

 Activity 5.2

What do you think an employer wants from the interview? Tick the ones you agree with.

a To look at you ☐

b To see if you match up to your application form ☐

c To check what you know about the job ☐

d To have a friendly chat ☐

e To find out why anyone would want to study nutritional biochemistry with Serbo-Croat ☐

f To see if you are basically suitable for the job ☐

 Activity 5.2 – comments

These may all be valid reasons for wanting to interview you, except for **d**. Recruiters, these days, can't afford 'friendly chats'. There's a purpose to everything, so don't think that 'the gift of the gab' will get you a job without very careful and thorough preparation to back it up. Let's look at the other reasons.

a The way you look does matter. If you didn't tick this, remember that the impression you make is based on a number of things including your appearance. We will look at the 'non-verbal' aspects of an interview later.

b I'm sure you ticked this. Getting an interview means that you did a good written application – now you've got to live up to it, expand on the information and show off your communication skills.

c Here's where all that research in the Careers Service pays off!

e OK, it's unlikely that an employer would interview you just for this alone, but s/he certainly will be checking out the details of your course, since there is so much scope for 'optional extras' these days.

f Absolutely! This is the real purpose of the first interview and it takes in all the preceding reasons plus a few more.

For example:

- to talk about your work experience;
- to see how well you respond to 'difficult questions';
- to get some idea of your personal qualities;
- to talk about your interests;
- to give you a chance to 'sell' yourself.

 Activity 5.3

Are there any other things you can think of that an employer might want from an interview? Note them down now.

Most employers will have some kind of checklist to fill in after the interview – some are more structured than others. This not only helps them to remember who you are, when they get back to the office, but it also allows the interviewers to assess candidates on the same criteria. This is particularly important when the forms are passed on to someone else who was not in on the original interview, but who has to make decisions about second interviews.

So, let's look at one example of a typical interview evaluation form.

Appearance and manner Suitably dressed? Neat? Any curious mannerisms? Facial expressions? Confident? Diffident? Eye contact?	Excellent Adequate Poor **A** | **B** | **C** | **D** | **E** Comments:
Preparation into company and job Read company recruitment literature? Company report? Read about type of work in Careers Centre handouts?	Excellent Adequate Poor **A** | **B** | **C** | **D** | **E** Comments:
Preparation on self Your course? Experience? Ambitions? Reasons for applying, etc? Motivation for job?	Excellent Adequate Poor **A** | **B** | **C** | **D** | **E** Comments:
Self-expression Clarity, speed and audibility of speech? Explanation of ideas?	Excellent Adequate Poor **A** | **B** | **C** | **D** | **E** Comments:

I could show you more of these forms, but it is enough to know that the interviewer is looking for certain attributes and that all candidates will be judged in the same way. Obviously, 'chemistry' or 'gut reaction' can never be ruled out, nor can you totally eradicate personal prejudice, but those things are out of your control. Let's deal with what you can control or at least what you can prepare for!

What do you want from the interview?

But what about you, the candidate? Don't you have needs too? If you are going to prepare effectively, you should understand what you want out of the interview. Yes, OK, obviously a job or a place on the course. But what do you want to achieve in the short time you have with a selector?

Here is a possible checklist:

a   To create an *impression* – a positive one that will stay in the selector's mind.

b   To *market your suitability* for the job by presenting relevant information about yourself and your experience.

c   To *collect information* in order to make a sound decision.

None of the above can be achieved by a passive attitude. *Active participation* is the key to a mutually satisfactory selection interview.

The format of the interview

We tend to think of an interview as one-to-one, and this is probably the most common form it takes. Selection is a very costly business for organisations, so there has to be a good reason for having more than one person involved. But it does happen.

Anyone who has applied to the Civil Service will tell you about the *panel* experience – six to ten people arranged at a long table facing the solitary candidate's chair! Similar arrangements happen in teaching, social services, academic posts, etc, but the panel is normally smaller – maybe two to four members.

A panel interview will not make any difference to your preparation, but it will mean extra flexibility in your responses to questions. All the panel members have a reason for being included and they probably each have a 'pet' subject. You won't know this beforehand so you will probably find that the interview doesn't flow in the same way as a one-to-one. It's not easy building a rapport with five people at the same time! We will discuss your response to a panel interview in Chapter 7 on pages 58–63.

Bear in mind that panel interviews become more common as you progress through your career, so even if you haven't met one yet, it's lurking round the corner!

Equal opportunities

 Activity 5.4

Write a definition of equal opportunities.

Difficult? This is something you need to think about. Equal opportunities is now the *corner stone of all good recruitment practice*. This obviously means that you should not be asked offensive or discriminatory questions. If you feel that a particular question is discriminatory or that the whole tone of the interview is suspect, then you do have the right to comment.

Remain calm and rational and ask about the relevance of a question or enquire about the company's equal opportunities policy. The more people who do this, the less common it will become. Remember also what I said about good recruitment practice – many organisations will not appreciate the importance of equal opportunities and this will show in the way they conduct their selection.

It is common now in the public sector to be given an equal opportunities interview, sometimes as the only one or sometimes as a supplementary one. This serves the dual purpose of checking out your own attitude and beliefs about equal opportunities, and also satisfies the organisation's selection requirements. Practice does vary, but you may be given a series of questions in a set format, in a neutral tone and with no verbal or non-verbal feedback from the interviewer. This ensures that no candidate has preferential treatment. The intention is good; the practice is extremely unnerving if you don't know what's happening. We all look for reaction from our interviewer – this is rather like being interviewed by remote control in a box!

Summary

Understanding the purpose of the interview is crucial. By knowing what the employer wants and what you want from the proceedings you can start to plan your strategy.

Which is what we're going to do next.

6 Practical preparation

You put a lot of work into your written application, didn't you? Well, now is the time to revise it all. Find your applications file (and if you haven't got one, make one *now*) and take out the photocopy of your application form and the graduate brochure etc.

Let's run through the procedure again.

a Read the brochure noting details of company organisation, job functions and particular requirements.
b If there wasn't a brochure, where did you research the company?
c Read the job description and make sure you understand the tasks involved in the job.
d Draw up a person specification from the details given, especially relating to skills, qualities and personality.
e Check whether the Careers Advisory Service has a video on the company. By the way, you did attend the presentation, didn't you?
f Read your application form through and jot down what specific skills and experience you mentioned and what examples you used.

Now you are ready to start predicting the questions.

Predicting the questions

Every interview you experience will be different, but your selectors will share common concerns. As a graduating student, you can predict certain areas of questioning and, having predicted them, you can thoroughly prepare for your answers.

 Activity 6.1

Make a list of topics you would expect to come up in an interview for a graduate job.

Can you, even at this early stage, begin to put these topics into categories? For example, do you have several topics relating to your education or your work experience? Before I help you to expand this list, see if you can create categories and then fit your suggested topics into them.

 Activity 6.1 – comments

You may have found that your categories mirror the normal sections of a CV or application form. This is very understandable as the interview normally follows a successful written application and will, therefore, continue and expand the same areas. This also reinforces what I said earlier about revision of your written application. So you can see that for part of the interview you are on safe ground.

Have a look at a sample of 'expected' questions.

a Why did you choose to take a qualification in ...?
b What benefits have you derived from your education?
c What aspects of your degree/diploma/etc are most relevant to this job/course?
d What do you hope to be doing in five years' time?
e What are your strengths and weaknesses?
f Tell me about your most relevant work experience.
g What do you enjoy doing in your spare time?
h How did you find out about our company/course?
i Why do you think you are suited to a career in ...?
j Why have you applied to us?
k What skills do you think you will need for this job?
l How would your best friend describe you?
m How does this course fit into your future career plans?

Now, let's move from the general to the more specific. When you attend an interview, you will normally have submitted something in writing beforehand. You can assume that your interviewer has read this. So, as well as the general questions which relate to every student, there will be particular points from your application to be covered.

 Activity 6.2

For this next exercise I have provided you with a job description and a completed application form (see pages 54–57). Look at the form with an employer's eye. First, are there any gaps or inconsistencies you would want to clarify? Note them down now.

Secondly, why would you want to interview this candidate? What is offered over and above the expected? If you have worked through Part A, on written applications, you will know that there is an emphasis on giving evidence both of experience and skills. What parts of this application form would you want to examine at interview? Write them down.

Lastly, take this a step further. Pick one of the above and think up a couple of questions which would encourage a candidate to give you more information.

Now you know how hard it is to be on the other side of the desk! Looking at your application form with an employer's eye is an excellent way of predicting likely questions.

Another source of possible questions lies in the brochure or job description. You will have used all this information in your application already, and you will now be revising this for interview. Again, assume that you are the employer. Look at the job description provided and think whether this suggests 'extra' questions. I'll give you an example:

> '..... *our aim is to give you middle management responsibility as early as possible.*'

Using the behavioural interview model, you would now be looking for evidence, from the past or present, of an ability to take on responsibility. So in the case of this applicant, you might want to check out how much of the work experience was 'undirected' and whether there was scope for initiative. You might even want to challenge the interviewee to produce evidence, since there is no mention in the form of positions of responsibility.

 ## Activity 6.3

Look at the job description and pick out the most important requirements of the job (you will have done a similar exercise already if you have completed Chapters 2 and 3). If you were interviewing for this job, what would be on your checklist?

Now, for each of the items on the list, look for evidence in the application form and tick if you find any. When you've finished, there will probably be items unticked, or perhaps queried, if the evidence is slim. These will form the core issues to be addressed in the interview. My own analysis follows.

Key requirements

- intellectual ability
- relevant work experience
- character – lively personality, an 'individual'
- common sense
- flexibility
- eye for detail
- leadership ability
- communication
- physical/mental stamina
- judgement skills

- takes responsibility
- rises to challenges
- ambition
- problem-solving

So, if I were interviewing Sheila Brown, I would now have an idea of how far she matches my requirements and of where any weaknesses may lie. I would also have earmarked some topics for further discussion. Now I'm ready to map out my questions. Are you ready to answer them?

Trick questions

Is there such a thing as a trick question in an interview? Can you define what it means to you?

 ### Activity 6.4

Give me an example of a trick question you've experienced. Or if that's not possible, can you think of what you'd describe as one?

 ### Activity 6.4 – comments

Now why is that a trick question? Here are some of the examples people give:

'He asked me something really technical about my subject which I couldn't answer.'

'She said that an English degree was pretty useless and what relevance could it possibly have?'

'I happened to mention that I belonged to the Student Union, and the interviewer was very aggressive about my political activities.'

'She said "Suppose that you are a store manager. It's 8 o'clock on a Friday morning and your main delivery lorry has overturned on the M1, leaving your shelves rather bare in two sections. What would you do?" How could I answer that – I'm not doing the job yet!'

' "What would you say was your main weakness" – do they really want to know?'

'He kept on and on about my A-level repeats and whether I would cope with professional study.'

'She said "I'm surprised that you are interested in accountancy with a Social Science degree – I thought you'd go for public sector work."'

' "Why should I appoint you," she said, "when I have hundreds of applications from people with relevant experience?" '

' "Tell me how you feel about the removal of the binary divide" – I didn't know what on earth it was.'

' "Since you've applied to the NHS, you must have strong views about the present re-structuring." Since I didn't know what his views were, I was afraid of giving a wrong answer.'

'So, how did you feel the interview went?'

For trick questions read tricky questions. Most interviewers do not try to catch you out – despite the horror stories you hear. But they do try to challenge you. They need to check out how you respond under pressure and whether you can put together a calm rational answer to provocative questions. Leaping across the desk and grabbing the interviewer by the throat will not impress upon him your great negotiating skills!

Should you be asked questions which you do not understand, then say so and ask for clarification. Don't waffle on and hope nobody notices.

Tricky questions still draw on the preparation you have done on the company and on your own suitability for the job. Be calm, be flexible and don't rise to what you see as an implied insult. Even the political questions are in there for a purpose – to check your understanding of current topical issues and to see whether you can argue your case rationally. There is no wrong answer – except, obviously, one which is blatantly discriminatory in some way.

'Tell me about yourself'

When you go into an interview, you expect to be asked questions. I've spent a lot of time in this chapter talking about preparation for questions and how this can make you feel much more confident.

So, you walk into the room, feeling calm and confident, but anticipating some challenging questions. What does your interviewer do? Sits back in the chair, looks you full in the face, smiles and says 'Well, Ms ..., tell me about yourself.' The sheer panic which follows chases every rational thought out of your head as you struggle to string a few coherent phrases together.

It's just not fair, is it? Answering tricky questions – OK. But having to talk, unprompted, about yourself, so early in the interview – well, that's just not cricket! It does happen, however, and you can prepare for it. Let's think it through.

 Activity 6.5

What is the purpose of this kind of approach? Jot down your first thoughts.

Did those thoughts include tactic as well as content? This is not just a lazy interviewer who hasn't done his homework and doesn't have any questions to ask. The strategy is clear:
- to judge whether you can think 'on your feet' and put together a coherent resume;
- to give you an opportunity to 'sell' yourself.

If you accept that there is a purpose behind this question, then you need to decide what your priorities are in answering it. Where would you start? What will you include?

 Activity 6.6

Begin by noting down what you would want to include.

Now think about the order. Will it be chronological or will it reflect your priorities? Bearing in mind that there is no right or wrong answer to this, but that you must be clear of your intentions, try to draft an answer to this question.

Now, read through your answer. Have you missed any important issues? Remember that you cannot include every single detail of your education, work experience and interests, but rather you must centre on the 'selling points', and in a fairly short space of time. Also, what you say now may dictate the direction of the interview – don't include things which you don't really want to talk about.

Do you want to add anything or change anything?

At this point, look at your response with an interviewer's eye. What would you have learned, over and above the facts (many of which will be on the application form)? Any inklings of personal qualities? Reasons for wanting the job? Company knowledge?

Activity 6.6 – comments

Here are two possible answers based on the application form on page 54. The approach is different in each.

a

I'm 22 years old and I come from Treesbury in the West Midlands. At present, I'm studying for a Combined Arts degree at Middletown University. This combines English and German and allows me to include other subjects like philosophy and psychology. I've enjoyed the course very much and I think that my language will be particularly useful in the future.

In my spare time I belong to a writers' group and I'm very interested in 'rap' poetry – in fact, this was the subject of my dissertation. I also enjoy sport, but not at a competitive level.

After my degree, I want to go into retail management and that's why I've applied to your company. I've got quite a lot of experience, both with M&S as a sales assistant, and with Landers Mail Order, so I'm very keen to do a graduate training scheme and learn every aspect of management. At the moment, I'm not absolutely sure where I want to end up, but I've enjoyed my experience of customer relations and also of market research, so maybe promotions or marketing might suit me.

I'd also like to use my German in the future – I've already spent some time working in Germany, so I'm familiar with commercial concerns over there.

b

Well, I'm considering a career in retail management after I finish my degree at Middletown University and that's why I've applied to Universal Stores. I feel that I have some insight into the industry through my work experience at M&S and Landers, and your graduate training scheme is an ideal way of learning about all aspects of management.

My degree is not directly relevant to this position, but it's given me very good communication and organisational skills – you have to be very self-disciplined to get assignments in on time. I've also worked in groups throughout the course and I like to be a member of a team. The degree is mainly English and German and I have spent some time working in Germany.

In my spare time I play sport, but not at a competitive level. My main interest is in writing and poetry. I belong to a local writers' group in Middletown and last year I organised the programme of events, inviting local poets to come and talk. I managed to combine this interest with my academic work by choosing to do a dissertation on 'rap' poetry. This was fascinating as it involved not only a critique of the poetry, but a study of the poet himself through interviews with his family and friends. I discovered that I'm actually very good at 'managing' a discussion in order to gain the information I need as quickly as possible. This should be a really useful skill in customer relations.

These are not model answers, there are good and bad points about both. What is important to note is that in each case there is an attempt at a rational approach – a starting point, a logical development and a real attempt to bring in relevant information as quickly as possible.

 ## Activity 6.7

Write down your own thoughts about these two examples, and compare them with your own answer.

'Is there anything you would like to ask me?'

As you do your preparation for interview by reviewing the job description and the company brochure you will become aware of 'gaps' in your knowledge. You may not fully understand the training schedule. You may be unclear about the amount of relocation to expect in the first few years. In some cases, you may be totally in the dark over the salary. These 'gaps' will form the basis of any questions which you may need to ask at the end of the interview.

 ## Activity 6.8

Write down a few things which you feel may generally be good to include.

Since interview performance is all to do with 'selling' yourself, you cannot afford to miss an opportunity. Are there things you know about the company/organisation which you could slip in: eg press reports about overseas expansion or Government white papers etc? Asking intelligent and *relevant* questions about topical issues can earn you a few brownie points. So can intelligent listening. If, during the course of the interview, you have gleaned some new and interesting information, then feed it back at the end, eg 'You were talking earlier about a possible expansion into .... Could you tell me a little more about this?' Or 'Would I be right in assuming, from your earlier comments, that your organisation anticipates some changes to its training programme?' Very clever stuff, that! Not only does it show that you were listening, but it boosts the morale of the interviewer no end – someone who finds his comments interesting!

Finally, don't overlook this part of the interview as a way of bringing in important facts about yourself which haven't yet had a chance to emerge. Far better to take the initiative and give the interviewer some positive insights, than to walk away and grumble 'He didn't give me a chance to talk about my Student Union work.' Hard luck! Come on, start taking control. We are talking about your future here.

Job description

'We bring people into real jobs because the only way to understand what retailing and management involves is through experience. Supported by individual formal training, seminars and tutorials, our aim is to give you middle management responsibility as early as possible. This level of management provides the basic training for many aspects of retailing as well as the chance for the ablest to show how their careers might be developed further. Many of our senior posts in general management, in central buying and in central departments, are filled by graduates.'

The graduates we need

'Degree discipline is not important. Personal qualities and skills are, however. We also welcome graduates with up to four years' previous work experience, not necessarily in retail. We need graduates with lively, practical, trained minds; with character and common sense, flexibility and an eye for detail. Leadership and the ability to communicate are fundamental management skills. Physical and mental stamina are both invaluable, as are the less easily defined attributes of discernment and taste.'

You and the partnership

'A great deal of attention is paid to personal development. There are a number of in-house management courses available, covering areas such as basic managerial skills, staffing and interviewing. Progress is monitored and constructive feedback encourages you to reach your full potential. Pay and performance are directly related.

'We can offer you the chance to work in a friendly, enthusiastic atmosphere, the opportunity to prove your ability through taking on as much responsibility as you can handle at an early stage, and the stimulation of a long-term career with us.'

Standard Application Form (SAF)

Please complete this form in BLACK ink or typescript.
Check employer literature or vacancy information for
correct application procedure

AGCAS/AGR
approved form

Name of Employer	UNIVERSAL STORES

Current/~~Most Recent~~ University/~~Polytechnic/College~~
MIDDLETOWN UNIVERSITY

Vacancies or training schemes for which you wish to apply
Job function(s)   Locations(s)
RETAIL
MANAGEMENT

First names (BLOCK LETTERS)   SHEILA

Surname (~~Dr, Mr, Mrs~~ Miss, ~~Ms~~) (BLOCK LETTERS)
BROWN

Out of Term address (BLOCK LETTERS); give dates at this address
149 PRINCES ROAD
TREESBURY, W. MIDLANDS
Postcode TR3 4BA   Telephone 01324 468201

Term address (BLOCK LETTERS); give dates at this address
SEDGEWICKHALL, MIDDLETOWN
UNIVERSITY, MIDDLETOWN
Postcode M28 3PP   Telephone 01222 414141

Date of birth	Age	Country of birth	Nationality/Citizenship	Do you need a work permit to take up employment in the UK?
3.3.70	22	ENGLAND	BRITISH	NO

Secondary/Further Education
Name(s) of Schools(s)/College(s)

	From	To	Subject/courses studied and level (eg GCSE, O, A, AS, H, IB, BTEC) Give examination results with grades and dates
TREESBURY COMPREHENSIVE	1981	1986	GCSE (1986) MATHS (C) ENGLISH (B) BIOLOGY (C) CHEMISTRY (D) PHYSICS (D) GEOGRAPHY (C) GERMAN (A) TECHNOLOGY (C) ENGLISH LITERATURE (B)
ARBOUR COLLEGE OF FURTHER EDUCATION	1986	1988	A LEVELS (1988) ENGLISH (C) GERMAN (B) SOCIOLOGY (D)

First degree/diploma
University/~~Polytechnic/College~~

	From	To	Degree/diploma (BA, HND, etc)	Class expected/ ~~obtained~~	Title of degree/diploma course
MIDDLETOWN	1989	1992	BA	2:1	COMBINED ARTS

Main subjects with examination results or course grades to date, if known

YEAR 1: ENGLISH, GERMAN, PSYCHOLOGY, PROFESSIONAL STUDIES
(OVERALL : 63%)
YEAR 2: ENGLISH, GERMAN, PHILOSOPHY OF RELIGION
(OVERALL : 58%)
YEAR 3: ENGLISH, GERMAN

Postgraduate qualifications
University/Polytechnic/College

	From	To	PhD/MA/ Diploma etc	Title of research topic or course
N/A				
				Supervisor:

Detail any scholarships, awards or prizes won at School and University/Polytechnic/College

N/A

Describe any aspect of your course of particular interest to you and/or of relevance to application

During the 3 years of my degree course, I have followed a module of I.T., which has allowed me to become familiar with Word Perfect and basic programming. For an Arts student this is an extra skill which will be useful in a commercial career. Also, my final year dissertation is on 'rap' poetry and I have conducted interviews with local residents for this.

Any other qualifications/skills, eg knowledge of foreign languages (indicate proficiency), keyboard skills, computer literacy

Word processing (Word Perfect), Basic programming
Fluent German.

Current driving licence?	Yes	No

Activities and Interests
Give details of your main extra curricular activities and interests to date. What have you contributed and what have you got out of them? Mention any posts of responsibility

My main interest has always been English literature, particularly modern poetry, and I read extensively. I am an active member of a local Arts Centre writing group. We meet regularly to discuss writing and also to read our own work. As chairperson, last year, I was involved in arranging the programme of speakers. This group is not university based, so it has brought me into contact with a wide range of local people. On a more active level, I play badminton with friends and I enjoy swimming. Although I have never reached team standard in these sports, I feel that they have contributed to my social life at university and also helped to keep me fit.

Work Experience Name of Employer	From	To	Type of work, including sandwich placements, vacation and part-time work. Include voluntary work.
Marks & Spencer	1986	1988	Saturday sales assistant
Ruhr Gas AG, Essex	Jul 1988	Mar 1989	Clerical work in Customer Relations Department
Landers Mail Order	1989	1992	Summer vacation work — mainly clerical in Direct Marketing Dept.

Which parts of this experience were most beneficial to you, and why?

At first my job with Marks & Spencer was just a Saturday job, but I gradually became more interested in retail sales, particularly the way stores are organised. My experience gave me an insight into customer relations and was often quite demanding for a teenager! At Landers I saw a different aspect of sales via mail order and I was fascinated by the market research that went into the catalogue production.
I certainly learnt some very important business skills.

3

Career choice

Explain what attracts you about the type(s) of work for which you are applying and offer evidence of your suitability

As my work experience shows, I have had a long-standing interest in retail. Over the years, my interest has changed from the 'sales' function to the organisation and marketing of goods. I am particularly keen to do management training with Universal Stores because it combines shop and direct marketing experience. My work references will show that I am hard-working and motivated, and that I mix well with people of all ages and backgrounds. Although I have received no business training in my degree, I feel that I am capable of learning new skills quickly. The retail business is essentially 'people-oriented', and this has always been an important consideration for me in my choice of career.

Please mention any points you wish to raise at interview

Future opportunities to move into direct marketing

Re-location

Do you have any restrictions on geographical mobility and/or a strong preference for a particular location? If so, give details

No, I am prepared to move anywhere in the UK.

If you feel there is anything which has not been covered adequately elsewhere on your application, please elaborate below.

I am very keen to carry on with study and perhaps gain professional qualifications, related to business or marketing. Also my fluency in German and my experience of working abroad may prove useful in future trade expansions with the EC.

Have you any family connection or other contact with this organization? If so give details

No

Health matters of possible relevance - colour blindness, etc.

I am in good health

Dates not available for interview

9-23 July

Date available for employment

From August 18th

Referees, one of whom should be academic. Give name, address and occupation (BLOCK LETTERS)

1 DR S.E. PETERS
SENIOR LECTURER
DEPT. OF ENGLISH STUDIES
MIDDLETOWN UNIVERSITY
MIDDLETOWN
Postcode M28 3PP   Telephone 01222 414141

2 MS J. ATKINS
OPERATIONS MANAGER
DIRECT MARKETING
LANDERS MAIL ORDER LTD,
DEVONSHIRE DRIVE
TREESBURY, W. MIDLANDS
Postcode TR2 8SA   Telephone 01324 710000

Date 23.5.92

Signature Sheila Brown

4

Careers Services are concerned to ensure that applicants are treated fairly and within the law. Many employers are now monitoring applications to help ensure that their recruitment procedures do not lead to discrimination. They also wish to ensure that they are meeting their obligations under various Acts of Parliament and related codes of practice concerned with race discrimination, sex discrimination and the employment of registered disabled persons.

These questions are designed to assist in this monitoring. They are placed in a separate section to emphasise that they relate only to monitoring and not to selection.

Employers who wish this section to be completed will generally notify this in their recruitment literature or in their vacancy notifications.

---

1 Sex   ~~Male~~   **Female**   (Please delete as appropriate)

---

2 Ethnic Origin   Please use this section of the form to indicate the ethnic group to which you belong or from which you are descended.
The ethnic origin categories are those recommended by the Commission for Racial Equality and used in the OPCS census.

[✓] White

[ ] Black Caribbean

[ ] Black African

[ ] Black Other (Please specify)

[ ] Indian

[ ] Pakistani

[ ] Bangladeshi

[ ] Chinese

[ ] Other (Please describe)

---

3 Disablement

If registered under the Disabled Persons (Employment) Act, please state from your Green Card:
Registration Number

Expiry Date of Certificate

Date   Signature

THE ASSOCIATION OF GRADUATE
CAREERS ADVISORY SERVICES

Revised 1992

THE ASSOCIATION OF
GRADUATE RECRUITERS

PC83G

7 Performing well

Verbal behaviour

You will have noticed that so far we've talked mainly about preparing for the interview. I hope that you agree with me that this is the foundation of good interview performance. If you've done your homework you can go into the room feeling far more confident. And confidence is the key to performing well. But if interview success depends simply on preparation, then why do we all feel nervous and why do we sometimes mess it up?

Partly, of course, it's lack of practice. Think of some other activity which scared you the first time you did it, eg giving a presentation, asking someone out, getting your hands on a computer – all these things get easier the more you do them. Unfortunately, or fortunately more likely, we don't go for interviews on a regular basis. It happens now and then, so there's no chance of much practice. On occasions when you are attending interviews regularly, (eg the milkround), then your performance does improve dramatically over an intensive three- or four-week period.

But you can *learn* from experience and improve your performance. Even if you've not had many interviews so far, you will already have an idea of your strengths and weaknesses in this context.

 Activity 7.1

Work through the following list of skills and rate yourself on a scale of 1 to 5 (from 'not at all competent' to 'very competent')

Initiating conversations	1	2	3	4	5
Carrying on conversations	1	2	3	4	5
Speaking clearly and audibly	1	2	3	4	5
Expressing ideas fluently	1	2	3	4	5
Talking about yourself	1	2	3	4	5
Discussing your strengths/achievements	1	2	3	4	5
Demonstrating interest/enthusiasm	1	2	3	4	5
Discussing your weaknesses in a positive manner	1	2	3	4	5
Providing succinct but comprehensive answers	1	2	3	4	5
Seeking clarification	1	2	3	4	5

Asking for a few seconds to gather your thoughts for a difficult question	1	2	3	4	5
Saying 'I don't know the answer'	1	2	3	4	5
Dealing with apparently inappropriate questions	1	2	3	4	5
Disagreeing with the interviewer	1	2	3	4	5
Asking questions about the job/employer	1	2	3	4	5
Asking questions about your likely opportunities	1	2	3	4	5
Demonstrating a sense of humour	1	2	3	4	5
Demonstrating self-confidence	1	2	3	4	5

The examples in Activity 7.1 demonstrate verbal communication skills. Some people are naturally very good at communicating – in social situations, in seminars, in work – but cannot get it together in an interview.

For them, the experience mirrors the tyrant–victim relationship. From being a bright, articulate, confident, active person they become completely passive; responding and reacting, but taking no responsibility for what happens in those important 30 minutes. It's rather like *Mastermind* – spotlight on you, mouth goes dry, mind goes blank and someone batters you with questions!

It's not really like that, is it? Now that you understand the purpose of the interview, you can see how unhelpful it is to the interviewer if you adopt the passive victim role. They have to work twice as hard to get anything out of you and, if it's so difficult, they probably won't bother.

I used the phrase 'taking control' at the end of Chapter 6. That's a very extreme measure – though you may be tempted to do this with an incompetent or inexperienced interviewer who's almost crying out for help. 'Taking responsibility' is probably a better phrase. You've done all the preparation. You believe you are a good candidate (if not the best). So it's up to you to make the most of the opportunity. The techniques of performing well at interview are very similar to those learnt through assertion training. If you wish to read more about this, I have included a few relevant books in Chapter 9.

 Activity 7.2

Compare the following dialogues:

a I-er: *I see you've been involved in the Student Union. Still, I suppose* *that's quite common isn't it, since you've all got to be members?*

I-ee: *Yes, I suppose it is. But not everyone is actively involved.*

I-er: *Do you have any examples of positions of responsibility outside college life?*

I-ee: *Well, I've not really had the chance to do things off campus.*

b I-er: *I see you've been involved in the Student Union. Still, I suppose that's quite common isn't it, since you've all got to be members?*

I-ee: *Actually, the reason I put that down was because it has involved quite a lot of committee work, which I think is useful experience for someone hoping to go into personnel.*

I-er: *Right, tell me about that.*

Write some notes about the evidence of 'taking responsibility' in these two examples.

 Activity 7.3

Think how you might respond to the following comments:

a *Your work experience is not really relevant, is it?*
b *Has your degree contained anything vocational at all?*
c *It must be nice to be able to spend a year travelling around Europe.*
d *Mature entrants often have some difficulty fitting in to the office – the staff are nearly all under 30.*
e *You didn't do too well in your A-levels, did you? I'm not sure that you'd cope with the qualification study.*

 Activity 7.3 – comments

You could say that these are in the *tricky question* league, but they come at you almost as *throwaway* lines, effectively blocking any development. You need to challenge the *unspoken assumptions* or you will miss good marketing opportunities. Use the good old assertion technique: *'I understand why you might think that, but actually …'*

However you reply, don't admit a negative. For example, with question **b** you would seriously weaken your case by starting your reply *'No it hasn't.'* No matter what you go on to say, you can't take away that first word. Rather say *'I would consider many aspects of my course to be vocational. I've had the chance to develop good communication skills, to use information technology, research and process data and to work as a member of a team. These seem to be very relevant skills for your company training programme.'*

Non-verbal behaviour

To be successful at an interview, you need to reassure the interviewer that you are the best candidate for the job. This is as much to do with the way you act as with what you say.

I firmly believe that thorough preparation brings confidence – so that's your first goal.

 Activity 7.4

There are also some very easy practical steps to creating the right impression in the interview:

a Dress appropriately. What does this mean to you?
b Check out the geography. What do you need to know before you start out for the interview?
c Arrive in good time. Why?
d What are you going to do as you enter the room?
e Eye contact is extremely important. Why?
f You are allowed to smile. What effect does this have? Can you overdo it?
g What are you going to take into the interview? Why?
h What are you going to do with your hands? Is this a problem? (It isn't for most people.)
i How will you sit? Do you need to practise? (Coffee bar lounging can lead you into bad habits.)
j How can you show the interviewer that you are interested?
k What will you do at the end of the interview? (ie before you leave the room.)

 Activity 7.4 – comments

Are you feeling nervous already? This checklist is a way of making you aware of what's important. It isn't whether you wear blue socks or a plain white shirt (contrary to popular belief). These things are only important in so far as they make you feel comfortable and allow you to appear confident and relaxed.

Shaking hands, saying 'thank you', smiling, nodding and looking at the interviewer are simply extensions of our normal social behaviour. They help to put you and the interviewer at ease. But remember that this is a formal occasion, so behave accordingly and don't do anything to embarrass the selector.

Remember, also, that first impressions do last in people's minds. That should include everyone you meet in the building. The guy you swore at in the car park may be your prospective section head. It should also extend to any telephone contact you have with the organisation – be clear and polite at all times.

Do not rush off to the library to read every book they have on body language! You will end up never daring to move! Simply be aware of the way you present yourself. The more calm, efficient, pleasant and personable you appear, the easier it will be to convince your selector of your suitability. It gives you a head start.

If you are concerned about interview performance, check out what workshops are available at your Careers Advisory Service or watch their interview videos.

The de-brief

Every interview is a learning experience. To make sure that you get the most out of it, you should go over your performance mentally or talk to a friend as soon as possible afterwards.

 Activity 7.5

Keep this checklist until you go for interview and then answer the questions. Refer to it again if you anticipate attending a lot of interviews.

Interview checklist
  a How did you feel when you walked in? Why?
  b How did you feel when you came out? Why?
  c Write down any unexpected questions. Can you prepare for these next time?
  d Write down any new ways of asking questions, eg situational questions, 'different' questions: *'How do you think we should use this time?'*
  e Did the interviewer adopt any particular style, perhaps very informal, confrontational or impersonal? How did this affect you?
  f Which questions did you answer badly? Can you draft a better answer now?
  g Were there things you wanted to say but didn't get the chance to? How could you avoid this happening next time?

   h Were there obvious gaps in your knowledge?
   i Were you satisfied that you asked appropriate questions at the end of
      the interview? If not, what would have been better?
   j What did you say that impressed them?

 Activity 7.6

   Now write an action plan for next time. What did you learn and what will you
   do to improve your performance?

If you are unsuccessful, many organisations will offer you feedback. This is useful for
future preparation. You may identify a weakness in one area which can be overcome
before your next attempt.

8 What next?

In some cases, the next thing to happen is a job offer. Well done! Or maybe another more in-depth/technical interview.

In other cases, you will receive an invitation to an assessment centre for a one- or two-day programme of presentations, test group discussions and interviews. I don't intend to cover this subject now, as it is only applicable to certain sectors of employment. Your Careers Advisory Service has details of second stage interviews, so check them out in good time.

Remember: if at first you don't succeed ... Go for it again!

The very best success for the future!

9 Bibliography

Assertiveness

Dickson, Anne, (1982) *A woman in your own right*, London, Quartet Books. Specifically for women.

Fensterheim, Herbert and Baer, Jean, (1976), *Don't say yes when you want to say no*, London, Futura.

Hopson, Barry and Scally, Mike, (1989) *Build your own rainbow*, Leeds, Lifeskills Associates. User-friendly life planning.

Careers Advisory Service resources

Your Careers Advisory Service holds a great deal of information about self-assessment and job hunting, much of which is produced by AGCAS (The Association of Graduate Careers Advisory Services). The following material is particularly relevant:

Applications and Interviews. A very useful book containing hints on preparation for first- and second-stage interviews.

Tell me, Mr Dunstone. An informative and light-hearted look at the interview. (20-minute video.)

Two whole days. The second stage – assessment centre. (20-minute video.)

Check with your Careers Advisory Service about the availability of interview workshops and mock interviews.

Part C: Second interviews

Introduction

This part aims to provide an introduction to the format and content of the second stage of recruitment of new students. It will enable students to prepare effectively for assessment centres and to participate in the various tasks to the best of their abilities.

If you have never attended an assessment centre, or have been unhappy with past experiences, don't worry – the insight and practice that this part provides will increase your self-confidence and enable you to perform well.

Objectives

At the end of the exercises in Part C you should be able to:
- understand the purpose of the second interview and be familiar with different formats;
- prepare for certain standard activities;
- understand the use of group exercises and develop a personal strategy for these;
- make effective use of the information you gather in your decision-making.

This book is designed to enable you to work at your own pace, selecting the sections or exercises most appropriate for you at any given time.

In Part C you will be presented with information about second interview preparation and procedure and then questioned to check your understanding. You will perform exercises as you go through the text and these will form the basis of your preparation for any assessment centre which you may attend in the future.

The text includes quotes from students who have attended assessment centres recently. These should give you a real flavour of the experience and an insight into the feelings of your contemporaries towards this aspect of selection.

Good luck!

10 The second stage

When the letter arrives to invite you for second interview you can feel justifiably proud. You are now in the final 5 per cent of candidates – a real achievement. However, that first feeling of euphoria may well change to sheer terror as you read the details of what is to come.

Let's look back at what you've already gone through. First, there was the application form – remember that? You battled with questions about situations where you had to lead a group and questions about your life experiences and role models. Obviously you won that battle because you got a first interview!

So there you were, in your suit, waiting in the Careers Service or in the company foyer, secretly dreading the encounter, but keeping the fixed smile. Terrified? No, not you – just challenged! You answered the questions calmly and intelligently and you managed to 'sell' yourself to your interviewer by expanding on the application form and reassuring her of your supreme suitability. And it worked. They want to see you again!

So what can they possibly expect now?

Why do they want to see you again?

 Activity 10.1

Have a look at the list below and tick the likely reasons why they need to see you again.

a To get a second opinion ☐

b To see if you've got two pairs of shoes ☐

c To see you away from campus ☐

d To see how you respond to different challenges ☐

e To let you see the company ☐

f To give you a great time in a hotel with a free bar ☐

Well, in a way they are all possible, except for **b**. No one expects a student to have more than one decent pair of shoes to go with the interview suit!

By taking you away from familiar surroundings and putting you with a new group of people, selectors get the chance to observe you working and enjoying yourself. They entertain you in a hotel, give you dinner and drinks, so that you can relax and lose the stiffness of the one-to-one interview.

 ### *Activity 10.2*

Think about your first interview. Make a few notes about what you think the selector learnt about you in those 20 minutes.

 ### *Activity 10.3*

Now think about the job you've applied for and write down what else the selector might need to find out.

Obviously that first interview of 20/30 minutes wouldn't give the selectors a chance to see how you interact with other people and how you behave in a group. Nor was it long enough to check out thoroughly your knowledge of the job and your personal characteristics. You know yourself how the person who is great fun in the bar on a Friday night appears very different at the end of a long weekend walking in the wild. Familiarity may not breed contempt after two days in an assessment centre, but it will certainly allow the weaknesses – and the strengths – to emerge.

What to expect

 ### *Activity 10.4*

Different jobs have different needs. Compare the two jobs below and suggest what an employer might need to know about candidates for the jobs.
  a Personnel manager
  b Research scientist.

Are there significant differences? Are there common areas?

Some of the common areas might be:
  • intellectual ability
  • communication skills
  • job knowledge.

However, for the personnel manager an ability to interact well in a group may have a higher priority than for a research scientist. Similarly, degree content and technical skills would form the focus of the interviews for a research scientist but may be completely irrelevant to personnel management. Obviously these are generalisations, but this difference of focus may dictate a different second interview format for technical jobs.

A typical second interview programme for an R & D job for a chemical engineer may look like this:

Day 1	5.30 pm	Arrive at company guesthouse
	7.00 pm	Dinner with other interviewees and two company reps.
Day 2	8.30 am	Arrive at refinery
	9.00 am	Half-hour informal interview with an engineer
	9.30 am	One hour formal personal interview with two engineers
	11.00 am	One hour technical interview with two engineers
	12.00	One hour interview with Personnel Officer
	1.00 – 2.00 pm	Lunch with recent graduates
	2.00 – 4.30 pm	Tour of refinery and opportunities for questions
Or this:		
	11.00 – 12.00	Talk from MD about company and site
	12.00 – 2.00 pm	Lunch and tour of site with recent graduates
	2.00 – 4.00 pm	Four interviews
		1 Personnel
		2 Team Leader
		3 Postgraduate research assistant
		4 Head of Division

However, it is becoming increasingly common to build in group exercises even for research/technical jobs, since most graduates and postgraduates are expected to take on managerial/supervisory responsibilities as they climb the ladder. So another programme might look like this:

Day 1	1.30 pm	Arrive
	1.45 pm	Welcome and introduction
	2.00 pm	Presentation about company
	3.00 pm	Individual introductions
	3.30 pm	Break
	3.45 pm	Personality questionnaire
	4.30 pm	Group exercise – solving design problem
	5.30 pm	Company videos

	6.00 pm	Free time
	7.00 pm	Dinner with recent graduates and managers
Day 2	9.00 am	Technical interview with two engineers
	10.30 am	Personnel interview
	11.15 am	Management interview
	12.00	Lunch
	1.00 pm	Psychometric testing: verbal reasoning, abstract reasoning
	2.30 pm	Site tour
	4.15 pm	Depart

Pretty heavy stuff, one way or the other! Glad you're not a chemical engineer, are you? Well, hang on a minute. If you are applying for any management function, whether it be personnel, marketing, finance or suchlike, you are likely to have to go through similar programmes, only more so!

Here is a typical assessment centre programme for marketing candidates:

Day 1	6.30 pm	Arrive at hotel
	7.15 pm	Briefing session
	8.00 pm	Information meal with two young managers (not assessed)
Day 2	8.30 am	Arrive at Head Office
	8.45 am	Aptitude tests
	9.20 am	Mutual introductions
	9.50 am	Group discussions on a topic of the group's choice
	10.15 am	Coffee and preparation for Group Task
	10.45 am	Group Task: business situation
	11.25 am	Coffee and preparation for Interactive Case Study
	12.35 pm	Lunch
	1.45 pm	Opportunity to read company information
	2.15 pm	Talk on graduate training programme
	2.30 pm	Individual interviews
		1 Two selectors
		2 Interview with psychologist and discussion of test results
		3 Training Manager
	4.30 pm	Debriefing session
	5.00 pm	Finish

You can draw breath now. Yes, it is very intensive and very varied and if you get through the process successfully you will know that you deserve the job! But always remember what I said about first interviews: it is a two-way process. The second interview is normally held on company home ground and involves lots of different people. Use it as a way of deciding whether you like what you see.

 Activity 10.5

Jot down some of the things you might want to find out while you are there.

Let's turn this into an *aide-memoire* which you can photocopy and take with you on your visit. Remember you can add to this when you're there. For example, if the presentation mentions the choice between block and day-release, you might want to use your time in the bar to check out what type of training the recent recruits chose and why. The headings below are useful for jotting things under as they occur or in your free time at the end of the day.

What I want to know	How	When	What I found out

11 Preparing for a second interview

Now that you've had a chance to look at what might happen at a second interview, you will want to think about your preparation. With the first interview it was fairly straightforward – you can look back at Part B: Being interviewed. You revised everything that went into your application form and you attempted to predict areas of questioning. So what should you do this time around? Is it just a repetition of the first interview? Clearly, it is not. There will be panel or one-to-one interviews as part of the process, but there are all kinds of other activities, some of which would seem impossible to prepare in advance.

 Activity 11.1

Look again at the interview programmes in Chapter 10, pages 69–70. Place the activities into categories of *Can prepare* and *Can't prepare*.

Am I right in saying that your *Can't prepare* column is longer that your *Can prepare*?

OK, so your lists may be different from mine, but it does look as if much of the programme is unseen. There are reasons for this, which I will look at in a moment, and, more importantly, there are ways of maximising your potential!

But first let's look at the *Can prepare* items and run a checklist on those.

Can prepare

In this section we'll consider how you can use your time most effectively in the run-up to your second interview. The time you spend at an assessment centre will be packed with activities, interviews and socialising, so it will be difficult to find space for quiet contemplation and preparation – except when you're in bed and maybe this time is best spent sleeping!

Therefore, if you want to present yourself as a well-informed and well-prepared candidate, you've got to do your homework beforehand.

Presentations obviously need a great deal of time and attention, especially if you are relatively unused to giving them. But equally, introducing yourself in a concise and interesting way will benefit from a dry run. You will also be expected to show a greater insight, at second stage, into the job itself and the company/organisation, so you must do extra research and firm up on some of the generalisations which may have been acceptable at first interview. Remember, you're now in competition with the best candidates. Do yourself a favour and prepare well – as with exams, it will pay off in the end.

Personal introduction

There are several ways this can be organised. Sometimes you are given one minute to talk about yourself and sometimes it is turned into an ice-breaker exercise where you talk to a partner and then you introduce your partner to the group. However it is organised, you need to think about what you will include.

 Activity 11.2

Jot down what you would say about yourself. You might also want to try timing yourself. Many people don't realise how long a minute can be! Use a stopwatch and see how it feels. Always bear in mind the person spec. for the job you want – can you use this short time to project important information or qualities?

Remember, these may be the first words your assessors hear from you. Make it clear, concise and interesting. And don't mumble!

Company information/job knowledge

Obviously, as part of your general preparation, you will re-read the company brochure and any other information you managed to find. Further details will be given to you at the time of your second interview, perhaps in written form, perhaps also via talks, videos and tours. You will be expected to take in this information (so don't fall asleep), and it may possibly form part of the interview questioning. It is also important for you to be absorbing the company ethos and forming your own impressions. How do you feel about the style of presentations – can you see yourself working with these people? Do you think the company has given any thought to equal opportunities – are there any women managers involved in the assessment centre or representatives from ethnic minorities? Are you picking up any discrepancies between what you're hearing and what the brochure says? Are they talking down to you or treating you as an equal?

There is no way you can anticipate these details, but by doing your homework on the company beforehand you will be able to understand the new information more readily and ask intelligent questions about it.

Try to expand the base of your company knowledge before you attend. The brochure may just be enough to get you through the first stage, but now that you're so close to success, you need to go the extra mile. Read through everything in the Careers Service file, including Annual Reports – these may seem very dry but they can give you useful facts about expansion, turnover, product development etc. It may also be worth visiting your university or public library to see if they offer a press cuttings search such as McCarthy, or if they hold Extel cards. I've given you a list of sources in Chapter 13. Your interviewers will be impressed with any extra details you have discovered through your own efforts.

You will also be given a much greater insight into your chosen job area through contact with graduates and through the various activities. This may form the focus of your interviews – it may even be a time to discuss a change of mind, eg marketing > sales/finance > IT. Don't expect to get away with a woolly definition – it may just have got you through first interview, but it won't be good enough for the line managers and section heads. Ask questions, get yourself informed – these people are doing the job you want to do, use them.

Three things are required to catch the selectors' attention: well-reasoned and thoughtful directions in your CV history; enthusiasm for the job; close awareness of what the company requires from its employees as set out in the brochure.

Interviews

You have, no doubt, read Part B: Being interviewed. The preparation suggested in that part will be exactly the same for these one-to-one or panel interviews at the assessment centre. Expect more focus.

In addition to your application form or CV, this time the selectors will have notes from your first interview. In Part B I gave an example of a typical assessment form (page 42). These forms, with the interviewer's notes, are passed back to the Graduate Recruitment Office who use them as the basis for deciding who to invite to second interview.

By now, the selectors are forming a picture of your strengths and possible weaknesses. They will meet beforehand to discuss all the candidates and to share the information from first interviews. From this discussion they may draw up a shopping list for each candidate, eg:

'John is obviously very articulate and highly self-confident, but is he really committed to information technology? We know he's also applying for accountancy and finance work – where do his priorities lie?'

Or

'Mandy was very well informed about the job and the company and has some relevant work experience, but she seemed rather nervous at first interview – will she be able to cope with the pressure of our working environment?'

You need to think back to your first interview, and if you used the checklist I suggested in Part B, Activity 7.5, page 62, you will have some idea of the good points of the interview and also areas of weakness or gaps in your knowledge, which should be filled before your assessment centre interview. If John and Mandy were to think of their performance at the first stage they may be able to use their knowledge to improve things this time around, eg:

(John) 'They asked me where else I was applying and seemed a little surprised that I was interested in accountancy. I need to show a lot of enthusiasm for IT.'

(Mandy) 'I know I was nervous, but I think it got better as the interview went on. I really must make an effort to join in and state my opinions assertively.'

Well done, John and Mandy. Now how about you?

You will meet a variety of interviewers – personnel managers (usually different from the milkround), technical managers, occupational psychologists, section heads etc. Each will have his/her own particular interests, and if you have several interviews, expect some duplication of questioning. You may be encouraged to talk in more depth about relevant academic work or relevant experience. You will certainly be challenged to demonstrate your knowledge of the job and the organisation and, above all, you will be expected to sell yourself.

I've talked a great deal throughout this book about self-marketing or selling yourself. You have got to show yourself in the best light at an interview and particularly at an assessment centre, where your interpersonal skills are being judged throughout the two or three days. Just don't go over the top. If you watch the AGCAS video *Two whole days* you will see one character who makes an art of arrogance and self-satisfaction. Guess who didn't get the job! True self-confidence and assertiveness come from a respect for oneself and for others. Once you overstep the mark into a dominating, cocky or superior attitude with your fellow candidates, or with the selectors, your behaviour may be thought dishonest and offensive. Be true to yourself – show your good points, but don't hit people over the head with them!

 Activity 11.3

Interviews at assessment centres can also be used to feed back test results, personality questionnaires, profiles and observers' comments. Why do they do this?

Now write down three good reasons why the employer would share this information with you.

Did you think of three? Were they sensible? I'm sure they were. You know by now the kinds of qualities demanded of candidates by graduate recruiters and several of these can be checked out through this sharing process. For example:

- Communication skills: a chance to give clear, rational responses.
- Team-working skills: your ability to work with managers towards an assessment of your skills and development needs without being defensive.
- Self-confidence: this is your chance to argue your case, and if weaknesses are highlighted, to redress the balance.
- Self-awareness: were you aware of occasions when you didn't contribute as well as you could? Can you evaluate your overall performance and talk about the skills you showed in the various exercises, without resorting to hollow boasts or excuses (I wasn't at my best)?

Remember always that recruiters are looking for reassurance. Appointing staff is a risky business. The more confident you appear about your ability to do the job and the more open you are in discussions about your potential, the more likely they are to view you favourably.

It is useful to think broadmindedly and answer with well-reasoned, common-sense answers.

Presentations

For my purposes here, I will comment briefly on doing a presentation in the context of the assessment centre.

 Activity 11.4

Why do recruiters want to hear you give a talk? Tick which apply:

    a To see how clearly you speak ☐

    b To reject anyone from the North-West ☐

    c To check out whether you can switch on an OHP ☐

    d To see how logical you are in your planning ☐

    e To find out how much you know about a given subject ☐

Hands up anyone who said, 'What's an OHP?'

Presentation skills are very important to anyone contemplating a management or research job. Most recruiters will need to check out your skills either through a formal talk or through a group exercise presentation.

Answers **a** and **d** obviously reflect the concerns of the recruiters, as does **c** to a certain extent – although not all students have a chance to use audio-visual aids on their course and employers appreciate this. Answer **e** is a possibility if you are set a work-related topic or if you are presenting your research project, but in many cases the content of your talk is less important than how you present it. Apologies to all citizens of the North-West for answer **b**. Regional accents are not a problem. Anyway, who defines an accent as regional?

 Activity 11.5

So let's assume that you have been asked to give a five-minute talk on one aspect of your extra-curricular activities. What subject will you choose? Bear in mind the time limit – do you know enough about this subject to fill five minutes? Or the reverse – will you struggle to squash your vast knowledge into such a short time?

Write down the subject you have chosen for this exercise.

What is the main theme of your talk? For example, if you choose to speak about windsurfing, your main idea could be:
 – the Windsurfing Society at university
 – windsurfing equipment
 – the history of windsurfing
 – a typical day's windsurfing
 – your own involvement.
And so on.

One main theme is all you've time for, so write that down. Now think of three aspects of your main theme:
eg Subject: Windsurfing
   Main idea: My personal involvement
   Three aspects: 1 how I became involved
                   2 where I do it
                   3 how much it costs.

 Activity 11.6

Write down the three aspects you would cover in your talk.

Are you happy with those? If at this stage you are struggling to get an angle on your subject, then you still have time to try another one. Certainly if you are planning this presentation several weeks in advance, you may want to test out an alternative.

Write down a second idea.

I said earlier that recruiters are mostly interested in the way you plan and deliver your presentation. Hopefully the content will capture their interest, but offering them fascinating and erudite detail on the mating habits of the tree frog will not, in itself, win you brownie points.

You have, possibly, been on the receiving end of lectures from experienced, knowledgeable people, which have either sent you to sleep or left your head reeling. Aim to get your message across clearly and concisely – give your talk a structure.
- introduce yourself and your subject;
- outline the main content of the talk;
- give the talk, moving clearly from section to section (links);
- summarise what you've said and give a conclusion;
- ask for questions.

 Activity 11.7

Over to you now. Make some notes on your talk under the following headings:
- Introduction
- Outline
- The main talk in sections: a, b, c
- Summary and conclusion.

How did you do that exercise? Did you make notes or did you try to write it out longhand? This question leads on to a consideration of **how** you give your talk.

Here are a few summarised points about how to give a talk.
- Perform – don't read – your presentation.
- Use notes not a script.
- **Don't**: mumble, gabble, shout or be sarcastic.
- **Do**: keep audience eye-contact, explain, intrigue, keep it personal.

If you do decide or are encouraged to use audio-visual aids, think about their best use. There is very little point holding up a picture in a large room – wouldn't it be better to photocopy it on to an acetate or not use it at all? Badly used and badly presented audio-visual aids are worse than nothing.

 Activity 11.8

Now you're ready for a rehearsal – with the stopwatch or kitchen timer. Run through your talk several times, preferably with a friendly audience. Remember you'll probably speed up when you do it for real – most people speak more quickly when they're nervous. And try to anticipate likely questions. Don't over-rehearse, though, otherwise it will sound like something you know off by heart.

Summary

So there is a certain amount of preparation you can do beforehand. Doing this well will allow you to feel much more confident when you arrive at the assessment centre. However, you will remember that most of the activities noted in Activity 11.1 fell into the *Can't prepare* category.

Can't prepare

When you attend your first assessment centre, it may feel like walking into the unknown. It is difficult to imagine what it will be like and you will naturally feel apprehensive.

As you will discover from working through this section, recruiters use the unfamiliarity of the situation as a way of seeing the real you and of presenting you with new challenges. This may explain the mystique which seems to surround assessment centre practices. Of course, if you attend several of these affairs, you will become less apprehensive, but each occasion will be different and will contain new and unexpected activities, so the adrenalin will start to flow just the same. Don't allow yourself to become blasé!

 Activity 11.9

Let's look at the *Can't prepare* tasks now. First of all, why do you think recruiters want to put you through so many unseen exercises? Look at the reasons below and tick which ones you think likely.

a To see how you respond to pressure ☐

b To check out the personal qualities you claimed to have on the application form and in the first interview ☐

c To experience living with you for two days ☐

d To make sure you don't slurp your soup ☐

e To see how well you work in a team ☐

f To check out your stamina ☐

g To see how good you are at adapting to new situations ☐

You may have hesitated over ticking **c** or **d** but you are on show and rightly or wrongly, you will be judged in terms of the company image. So your social behaviour is important, but more of that later.

 Activity 11.10

> Are there other reasons for using unseen exercises? Write them down if you have thought of any not included in that list.

Recruiters can learn a great deal about you from watching you perform tasks in a group. It is the closest they can get to judging how you will do the job. Most organisations use occupational psychologists to design their group exercises, so that they can observe certain skills/qualities accurately. A typical list might include:

- drive
- competitiveness
- decisiveness
- self-confidence
- task orientation
- social skills
- communication skills
- debating skills
- logic
- quick thinking
- imagination
- speed in assimilating data.

I could add more, but it's enough to show you why these exercises are used and also to stress that you cannot presume to know what each recruiter is seeking. If you try to play up to an imagined agenda, you may go horribly wrong. If you dominate your group in the assumption that leadership skills are essential, then you may score nil on the team working/facilitating scale – and this may be more important to that particular recruiter. Hard cheese!

Let's look at these activities in greater detail.

Aptitude tests

I put a question mark after this item in my *Can't prepare* column for Activity 11.1. The reason being that you can only do a certain amount of preparation for aptitude tests by familiarising yourself with the format. For obvious reasons of validity, psychometric tests are not released to the general public – you are unlikely to see the actual test beforehand. Nor should you, since these are measures of ability and therefore should not be rehearsed. However, you can get hold of examples. I have mentioned some reference books in Chapter 13, but you can't beat actually doing some tests. Check out whether your Careers Advisory Service runs practice sessions.

 ## Activity 11.11

Set out below are some examples from the most common types of tests: verbal reasoning, numerical reasoning and diagrammatic reasoning. Have a go at these (the answers are in the appendix on page 102).

Example A: Verbal reasoning (*reproduced by permission of Saville and Holdsworth*)

Read the passage and consider the statements which follow it. Then mark the answer boxes according to the key. You must fill in only one box for each answer.

In a large town where the drink–driving laws are rigidly enforced, it was found that only 30 per cent of drivers breath-tested were completely alcohol-free during a certain period. Among those who were married, however, 50 per cent were completely alcohol-free during the same period.

   a Strict enforcements of the drink–driving laws did not prevent 70 per cent of drivers drinking some time during this period.

   b If drivers had to be married, their drink–driving record would improve.

   c Less than 30 per cent of those drivers who were unmarried were completely alcohol-free during this period.

A Clearly true
B Clearly untrue
C Cannot say/insufficient evidence

           A **B** **C**
a ☐ ☐ ☐
b ☐ ☐ ☐
c ☐ ☐ ☐

Example B: Quantitative reasoning (*reproduced by permission of BT*)

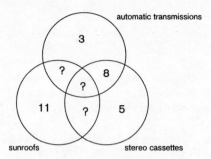

automatic transmissions

3

?   8

?

11   ?   5

sunroofs   stereo cassettes

Numbers of cars with refinements, manufactured by a small company in a short period, are distributed as follows:

a How many cars have automatic transmission but no other refinements?

b How many cars have a stereo cassette but no sunroof?

c Overall, 17 cars have two out of any of the three refinements. If 42 cars are manufactured altogether, how many have all three refinements?

Example C: Non-verbal diagrammatic reasoning

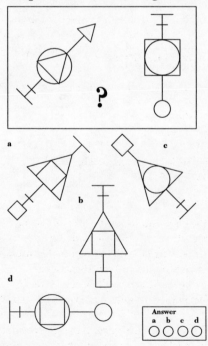

a

c

b

d

Answer
a b c d
○ ○ ○ ○

Example D (*reproduced by permission of ASE Occupational Division of NFER-NELSON*)

   a Which one of the five words on the right bears a similar relation to each of the words on the left?

1	2	3	4	5
Just Blonde	Light	Only	Unjust	Fair	Brunette

   b Which one of the five words on the right bears a similar relation to each of the words on the left?

1	2	3	4	5
Loud Hard	Noisy	Brittle	Soft	Difficult	Inaudible

   c Write down the number of the word which would come in the middle, if the words were arranged in order according to their meaning.

1	2	3	4	5	6	7
Paragraph	Letter	Book	Sentence	Page	Chapter	Word

   d Multiply the second whole number by the third decimal.
       1, .9, 2, 4, .8, .7, 8, .5

   e Hear is to see as listen is to . . .

1	2	3	4	5
touch	audit	see	feel	look

   f Backwards is to reversed as upside-down is to . . .

1	2	3	4	5
forwards	inside-out	rightside-up	converse	inverted

   g Give the next number of the series:
     1/2   2/3   3/4   5/4   5/6   7/6

   h The third number of this series is missing – what is it?
     6   12   ...   48   96

Don't worry if you found some of these questions hard – no one is expected to get every one right. The numerical tests tend to be the most feared – by all students. Even maths/engineering students sometimes struggle with the arithmetic through lack of recent practice. These tests may also use graphs and statistical tables – so if you are not familiar with such devices it may be worth looking at a couple of the suggested books – just so that you don't fall to pieces as you come face to face with a spreadsheet.

All such tests are timed, so you will feel under pressure. Just listen carefully to the instructions, stay calm and work as quickly and as accurately as you can. Finally, remember that tests are only part of the whole assessment procedure. For a very few jobs the results alone will determine your progress. For most positions, however, your scores will be discussed alongside other information, eg your performance in the group exercises, in order to give an all-round view of your potential.

Personality questionnaires

There is no preparation you need to do for personality questionnaires. I have mentioned one book of examples in Chapter 13, and occasionally your Careers Advisory Service may offer the Occupational Personality Questionnaire (OPQ), but such tests are costly and time consuming. Obviously there are no right or wrong answers – you answer truthfully.

So what is their purpose? Again, as with aptitude tests, these are used by occupational psychologists to identify certain traits or characteristics which are important to a given job. The profile from your marked questionnaire may be discussed with you in one of the interviews and your reactions sought. If you feel that the profile does not represent your personality then say so – such measures as these are not 100 per cent accurate.

 Activity 11.12

Here are two examples of personality questions. Have a go.

Example 1 (*reproduced by permission of ASE Occupational Division of NFER-NELSON*)

Which answer comes closer to telling how you usually feel or act?
Are you usually:
  a a good mixer, or
  b rather quiet and reserved?

In deciding something important, do you:
  a find you can trust your feelings about what is best to do, or
  b think you should do the logical thing, no matter how you feel about it?

If you were asked on a Saturday morning what you were going to do that day, would you:
  a be able to tell pretty well, or
  b list twice too many things, or
  c have to wait and see?

Example 2 (*reproduced by permission of Saville and Holdsworth*)

Mark the statement most (M) like you and the one least (L) like you out of each trio.

   a I don't feel that time is wasted on planning.
   b I feel uneasy in the company of unconventional people.
   c If I'm annoyed with someone I don't show it.

   a I find rowdy social evenings fun.
   b I always set my sights high.
   c I think it's important to preserve our traditions.

Now you think you've cracked this, don't you? You're saying it's obvious which statement they want you to tick. Is it? Take this example:

When you are given an assignment to be handed in on a date in three weeks' time, do you:

   a go straight to the library to find the books;
   b put it on one side until nearer the deadline;
   c set yourself a date for starting it then carry on with other work;
   d do it at the last possible moment before the deadline?

 Activity 11.13

Come on then, use the crystal ball and predict the right answer. (Didn't I just say that there are no wrong and right answers?) What is your choice? Why is that the obvious choice?

I can give you an indication of personality for each of those answers:

   a This person is well motivated and hard working.
   b This person is independent and can make decisions.
   c This person is good at prioritising.
   d This person works well under pressure and can cope with tight deadlines.

But my colleague might read very different things into these answers:

   a This person lacks confidence and needs to read every single book on the subject.
   b This person has no time management skills.
   c This person cannot juggle two balls at the same time.
   d This person is irresponsible and sloppy.

What's the best advice? Just *do* the things as they are natural to you, don't try and turn yourself into the psychologist.

Group exercises

Discussions

It is very common to include at least one group discussion as part of the assessment centre programme. This can be either *led* or *leaderless*. In most cases you will be given a topic to discuss, but occasionally the group has to choose one from a given number.

 Activity 11.14

> All such discussions are observed by members of the assessment team. Write down what you think your observers will be looking for.

Now look at this typical observer checklist.

Evaluate the candidate you are observing according to the following criteria. Please tick for each contribution to the discussion.

Name	Number of contributions
Initiating	
Seeking information/opinion	
Giving information/opinion	
Clarifying/elaborating/summarising	
Encouraging others	
Dominating	
Ignoring contributions	
Notes	

So it's not just how often you speak but what you say to help discussion along. In a *led* discussion one candidate will take the chair and the group will be expected to reach consensus by the end of the time limit.

 Activity 11.15

> Put yourself in the position of the Chair. How would you see your role? Write down up to five things which the observers might be watching for.

You obviously included leadership skills and probably summarising. Did you also think of encouraging everyone to participate, keeping the discussion on track, keeping an eye on the clock and possibly controlling a dominant team member?

Well done! You realise that being the leader doesn't mean taking over the group and doing it all yourself. If there is one golden rule to remember about any group exercise, discussions in particular, it is to take an active part and try to contribute fairly early. There's nothing worse than sitting in a discussion unable to break in because the others have thrown themselves into the topic and left you behind. Get stuck in – give the observers something to observe.

'They are assessing you all the time, so you have to start off with a positive attitude, especially in the group discussion when you have to project yourself and get your ideas across.'

Group tasks
These are often the most enjoyable and challenging part of the programme. They are more structured than the discussion and often involve reading and absorbing a great deal of information. Sometimes a leader is chosen and sometimes you play a role, but again the observers are watching you perform as a member of a team and have a checklist to complete.

'We had to make a "decorative brickstand"! It had to support a brick and look good. What more can I say!'

I'm going to give you an example of a case study – this one is a variation of the 'who is the most valuable person to keep alive' exercise. I've chosen this case study because the first part is an individual exercise, so you can sit down and work through it. At an assessment centre, you would then take your individual ranking into the group and the ultimate aim is for group consensus.

 Activity 11.16

Cave rescue – briefing
Your group is asked to take the role of a research management committee who are funding projects into human behaviour in confined spaces. You have been called in to an emergency meeting as one of the experiments has gone badly wrong.

Six volunteers have been taken into a cave system in a remote part of the country, connected only by radio link to the rescue hut by the cave entrance. It was intended that the volunteers would spend four days underground, but they have been trapped by falling rocks and rising water.

The only rescue team available tells you that rescue will be extremely difficult and only one person can be brought out each hour with the equipment at their disposal. It is likely that the rapidly rising water will drown some of the volunteers before complete rescue can be effected.

The volunteers are aware of the dangers of their plight. They have contacted the research hut using the radio link and said that they are unwilling to take a decision on the sequence of their rescue. By the terms of the research project, the responsibility for making the decision rests with your committee.

Life-saving equipment will arrive in fifty minutes at the cave entrance and you will need to advise the team of the order for rescue by completing the ranking sheet. The only information you have available is drawn from the project files and is reproduced on the volunteer personal details sheet. You may use any criteria you think fit to help you make the decision.

Volunteer 1: **Helen**
Helen is 34 years old and a housewife. She has four children aged between seven months and eight years. Her hobbies are ice-skating and cooking. She lives in a pleasant house in Gloucester and was born in England. Helen is known to have developed a covert romantic and sexual relationship with another volunteer (Owen).

Volunteer 2: **Tozo**
Tozo is 19 years old and a sociology student at Keele University. She is the daughter of wealthy Japanese parents who live in Tokyo. Her father is an industrialist who is also a national authority on traditional Japanese mime theatre. Tozo is unmarried but has several high-born suitors as she is outstandingly attractive. She has recently been the subject of a TV documentary on Japanese womanhood and flower arranging.

Volunteer 3: **Jobe**
Jobe is 41 years old and was born in Central Africa. He is a minister of religion whose life work has been devoted to the social and political evolution of African peoples. Jobe is a member of the Communist Party and paid several visits to the USSR. He is married with eleven children whose ages range from 6 to 19 years. His hobby is playing in a jazz band.

Volunteer 4: **Owen**
Owen is an unmarried man of 27 years. As a short-commission officer he spent part of his service in Northern Ireland where, as an undercover agent, he broke up an IRA cell and received a special commendation in despatches. Since returning to civilian life he has been unsettled and drinking has become a persistent problem. At present he is Youth Adventure Leader, devoting much energy to helping young people and leading caving groups. His recreation is preparing and driving stock cars. He lives in Brecon, South Wales.

Volunteer 5: **Paul**
Paul is a 42-year-old and has been divorced for six years. His ex-wife is now happily remarried. He was born in Scotland, but now lives in Richmond,

Surrey. Paul works as a medical research scientist at the Hammersmith Hospital and he is recognised as a world authority on the treatment of rabies. He has recently developed a low-cost treatment which could be self-administered. Much of the research data is still in his working notebooks. Unfortunately, Paul has experienced some emotional difficulties in recent years and has twice been convicted of indecent exposure. The last occasion was 11 months ago. His hobbies are classical music, opera and sailing.

Volunteer 6: **Edward**
Edward is 59 years old and has lived and worked in Barnsley for most of his life. He is general manager of a factory producing rubber belts for machines. The factory employs 71 people. He is prominent in local society, a Freemason and a Conservative councillor. He is married with two children who have their own families and have moved away from Barnsley. Edward has recently returned from Poland where he was personally responsible for promoting a contract to supply large numbers of industrial belts over a five-year period. This contract, if signed, would mean work for another 25 people. Edward's hobbies include collecting antique guns and he intends to write a book about Civil War Armaments on his retirement. He is also a strong cricket supporter.

Did you think any of them worth saving? If you can get a few friends to do this exercise as well, you can then move into the second part, which is the group task. If you managed to do that, how did it feel to have to break up your carefully considered ranking order for the sake of group consensus? Not very easy is it?

 Activity 11.17

What do you think the observers would learn about you from this exercise? Write down up to five things.

Now look at this assessment form.

Assessment form

Please try to make an assessment of the 'candidate' you are observing using the following criteria:

Acceptability
Personal style not likely to be abrasive to colleagues or clients.

Persuasiveness
Ability to make a persuasive, clear presentation of ideas or facts, convince others to

own expressed point of view, gain agreement or acceptance of plans, activities or products.

Problem analysis/critical thinking
Effectiveness in identifying problems, seeking pertinent data, recognising important information, drawing sound inference from fact and reasoning logically.

Judgement
Ability to evaluate data and courses of action and to reach logical decisions.

Decisiveness
Readiness to make decisions, render judgement and take action.

Initiative
Actively influencing events rather than passively accepting; sees opportunities and acts on them. Originates action.

Planning and organisation
Ability to establish course of action for self and/or others to accomplish a goal.
Please use the following grades in assessing your 'candidate':
A = Well above required standard.
B = Achieved an acceptable standard.
C = Showed some skills but failed to reach standard.
D = Well below standard.
E = No evidence or conflicting evidence.

One other possible surprise for you in this exercise is that you (or another group member) will be asked to present your decision and give reasons. So you can't nod off or leave it to the others, because the finger may point at you!

 Activity 11.18

Here is another example, this time of a more active group task. Your brief:

You are a member of the Graduate Recruitment Team for Chocolat, a leading confectionery manufacturer. It is nearing the time for the launch of the graduate recruitment campaign and you are looking for a fresh, dynamic approach. Your task is two-fold:

a Design a recruitment poster for university Careers Services, which carries the main message of the campaign notes.
b Compile a two-minute plug to be broadcast on campus radio.

Here are the campaign notes:

Chocolat, one of the leading manufacturers of confectionery in the UK (Choxaway, Choclettes, Ultrachox and Chickenchox), are looking to recruit 30 graduates on to their Commercial Management Training Scheme. Any degree discipline is acceptable, but applicants must have some commercial work experience. We want drive, determination, creativity and a go-getting personality. Fluency in a foreign language would be a bonus since we anticipate expanding rapidly into the European market with our new range of chocolate credit cards, Lollichox. We want only the best students.

I bet you're really tempted by this one, aren't you? Well, find a blank sheet of paper. Get some friends over (4–6 people is a reasonable number) and give yourself 30 minutes to complete one or other of the tasks.

How did that go? The great thing about this exercise is that you can be as outrageous as you want, so long as you cooperate well with your fellows and finish the task. Remember you may be asked to give a presentation to the assessors, so keep your objectives firmly in mind.

Good fun, this assessment centre stuff, isn't it? Listen to some other student comments about group tasks.

'It is important to be continually involved, to push your own ideas, but not to dominate, and to be receptive to the views of others.'

'Probably the most frenetic hour of my life. Very complex "game" in which you had to manage four trainees (who act as nasty as possible) as they move the counters on a giant draught board! Everyone is shouting, the phone is ringing, the intercom is bleeping! Good luck!'

*'Wilderness exercise. **Fun!** Six of us had to complete answers to questions about surviving in the wild and then compare answers and agree a group consensus. Some great discussions about the relative merits of putting batteries under your armpits! It's all about consensus, so be prepared to concede if you're not making any headway after trying to persuade the others that you're right!'*

Individual exercises

Although I've said that the emphasis at the assessment centre is on group activities, there will probably be one or two exercises which you do on your own.

A very common one is an in-tray exercise where you are given the contents of your in-tray (memos, letters and phone messages) and asked to prioritise, giving reasons. You will also be given extensive details about the company – key roles, organisation hierarchy, employee attitude surveys, personal files etc, to help you in your decisions.

At the end of the given time you must present your priorities to an assessor (usually one-to-one).

 Activity 11.19

Think about this activity. Which of the following qualities/skills can be assessed? Tick whichever apply.

a Time keeping ☐
b Planning ☐
c Logical thinking ☐
d Team work ☐
e Absorbing information ☐
f Working under pressure ☐
g Forward planning ☐
h Judgement ☐
i Speed reading ☐
j Self-confidence ☐
k Decision-making ☐

I'm sure you ticked them all except **d**. Even this can be checked out during your feedback because you may be asked how you would handle certain situations with colleagues, which may arise from your decisions. You can see that it's the closest they can get to seeing you actually do the job.

 Activity 11.20

Here is another individual exercise, which you can do now.

Visitation

Scenario

You are the General Manager of a Betterfoods Superstore. On Friday afternoon at 4.30 pm you receive a telephone call from your regional executive. 'The Chairman is visiting this region on Monday. He wants to visit your store as he hasn't been there since you've been in charge. The Chairman, the RMD and I will be arriving at about 10.00 am. It will be the normal Chairman's visit. You haven't done one before, so here are a few points – we'll want a complete store tour, front and back, and he'll want to meet all key staff and as many others as possible. Arrange coffee for us. We'll be leaving at about 12.30 pm. Do ensure the store is clean and fully stocked after Saturday.'

Action

1 Decide upon your aim.
2 Make a complete written plan.
3 Prepare a briefing to selected members of your staff.

Background information

1 Your store organisation is as follows:

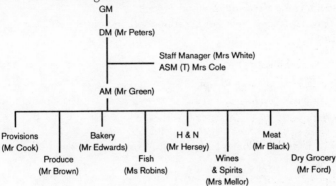

2 Your store has a sales area of 33,000 ft² and a back area of 15,000 ft.
3 Your turnover last week was £310,000. For the equivalent period last year it was £276,000.
4 You have 350 staff, of which 190 are part time.
5 Your staff turnover figure is 53 per cent.

Social events

All through your one or two days with a company they will spoil you rotten: good hotel, nice food, free bar, friendly and relaxed atmosphere! What have you done to deserve this?

They will also bring in young graduate trainees for you to talk to, so that you can get an insider's view.

'I'd say this was one of the most important "tests". Use the opportunities over a "few" drinks to chat to the selectors and the other undergraduates. This is where you make the biggest impression, when everyone is relaxed, but studying you very closely!'

Recruiting this way costs a company dearly, so they must think it's worthwhile. The fact that most large organisations still do it, despite the recession and the buyers' market, must mean that the style of the assessment centre is right. Treat you well, make you relax and then work you really hard the next day. Everyone will respond to that. But you do have some responsibilities. You are the guest for two days in someone's house. What are the no-nos?

 Activity 11.21

Write down up to five *don'ts*. Here are two to start you off.
1 Don't be rude about the food/service.
2 Don't smoke at meals or in groups without asking permission of the others.

I can tell you were well brought up! It's all common sense. Behave yourself and remember that even when they say you're not being assessed, such as at dinner, in the bar and so on, you are still making an impression. And these may be people you will have to work with at some stage. Oh, hello! Yes, I remember you. You were the one who said anyone would be mad to want to work in marketing! (Oh dear!)

> *'Although the dinner was very relaxed, we were informed that every manager present would be asked for his/her opinion of the candidates.'*

You may be wondering what to wear during these gruelling two days. Obviously you'll be working hard and you'll be involved in all kinds of activities, so you'll need to feel comfortable – *but* you are on show. Some companies will give you guidelines in their letter, eg Dress will be smart casual, but ties should be worn for the evening meal. Others will leave it to your discretion.

This is an interview, so dress accordingly. If you are travelling by train, you may want to wear something casual and then change as soon as you arrive. Take a change of shirt, tie or blouse, just in case of spillages, leaking pens or sweaty weather. It is worthwhile having something different to wear for the evening meal, especially for the women who may choose to wear a suit or skirt and blouse during the daytime. The evening meal will not be formal enough for a cocktail dress! You may, occasionally, be required to go on a tour of the office, factory or site – make sure your shoes don't cripple you!

Students are not expected to have an extensive wardrobe of formal clothes, but this is an important occasion so beg, borrow or even buy the right kind of clothes. As an investment, it will certainly pay off eventually.

Non-participative activities

That is not a very accurate title as you will want to be thoroughly involved in everything that happens, but these are things like company presentations, tours, videos and so on. You may feel inclined, in a busy schedule, to sit back and relax too

94

much on these occasions. Sorry, no snoozing in the back row! Stay alert – you may be asked for your comments later on. You may even want to talk during the interview about what you've seen and heard. It's a two-way process, as I keep saying. If you don't like what you see, then will you really want the job?

A good chance to get some candid answers from the people herding you around!

Summary

I hope that you now see how useful these unseen activities are to a recruiter. They can't put you in the job and observe you for six months before giving you a contract (shame!), so they have to simulate the kind of situations you might encounter or use exercises which allow you to demonstrate certain skills and qualities.

The majority of students who attend assessment centres really enjoy them – honest! The experience is demanding and is intended to stretch you and challenge you – not scare you out of your wits. It's your wits they want to see! So go along well prepared and throw yourself into the proceedings. Be seen as enthusiastic, lively, enquiring and ready to participate in everything (except, perhaps, the 'I can drink more than you and still be standing at 2.00am' game!). But remember – make a positive impression and learn as much as you can about the company and the job.

If you do all this you can relax on the train back home, and feel satisfied that you gave it your best shot.

12 What next?

Hopefully a job offer. Yippee! And usually very quickly. You will receive your offer by letter or even by telephone and you will be asked to respond.

Freeze the picture!

There you are, with the job offer in your hand. Will you accept? By this stage you should have a very good feel for the company and for the actual job you will be doing. You may be totally over the moon because you know that this is the job for you. So there's no problem – you write your letter of acceptance, confirming your start date and then wait.

It's quite likely that you won't get a formal contract until certain conditions are met: medical examination and satisfactory degree results (some employers will specify a class of degree) and so on, but if you accept in writing then you have committed yourself to the company and you should not be considering other jobs. It is very bad practice to renege on an acceptance without very good reason and it can get you into trouble (a word to a professional body could make life difficult if you apply to other member companies). So don't accept a job with the deliberate intention of rejecting it if something better turns up.

But what if you still have doubts? It's a good job – it may be the only offer you've had – it may be the only offer you'll get! Go on, take it! So what's being whispered in your other ear? You weren't really keen on having to move three times in the two-year training programme, were you? And you didn't like their response to the suggestion that you might be interested in doing an MBA, did you? Let's use a well-known mnemonic to check out this job offer.

S – surroundings (where will you work?)
P – prospects
E – environment (do you like the image of this industry/service?)
E – effects (lifestyle implications)
D – description of work
C – conditions
O – organisation
P – people

To be sure that you've got enough information to make the right decision you should have checked out each of these initials. If you haven't, how do you find out more?

Activity 12.1

Under each of the eight categories above, make a note of what you can do to find out more information.

You will have used each stage of the selection process to check out these things, so you are probably now looking at very specific concerns.

Here are a few suggestions:
- Ask to visit your office/section/site before making a decision. This way you can see exactly where you'll be working and with whom.
- Ring the Graduate Recruitment Office and ask them specific questions. If they can't answer, they will find out for you or refer you to another department.
- Talk to other people doing this job or similar work. How do they feel about this company?
- Re-read everything you can find about the company. Will you be proud to work for them?

'But if I'm waiting for the results of other interviews, what do I do?'

Most employers realise that good candidates may have several irons in the fire and they will respect this. Explain that you are committed to other interviews or awaiting results and negotiate a deadline for letting them know your decision. But then try to stick to this deadline – the employer will need to offer your job to someone else. Don't hog it if you don't want it!

'Now, I've got two job offers, which one shall I accept?'

Lucky you! Or possibly not-so-lucky you, as this can put you in a very difficult position. You may have been happy with either offer if they'd come separately, but when they come together ...? Decisions! Decisions!

Obviously you'll need to look carefully again at the jobs, the terms and conditions, training, future prospects and so on. If you're really stuck, it will help to talk to a careers adviser who will be objective and may put things into perspective for you.

Try a **SWOT** analysis. No, it's not a joke, it's a marketing technique! Divide a sheet of paper into quarters (see below) and for each job, write something in the boxes and then compare your findings.

Here's an example:

Strengths	Weaknesses
Good starting salary In London Day release for professional qualifications	Start date August – no holiday Very long hours – expected to work Saturday if necessary
Opportunities	**Threats**
Good chance of foreign placements Company is expanding into USA	If I want to move company, how acceptable is my training? There is nobody in the office over 35 – where do they go?

 Activity 12.2

Use blank SWOT forms when you need to make a decision.

There is a chance, of course, that you will not be successful on this occasion. As I said in Part B: Being interviewed, it is important to review each interview as soon as possible afterwards, so that you can note down any unexpected questions or gaps in your knowledge. This is equally true for second interviews.

Which activities did you enjoy? Which were a chore? Did you get involved in all the exercises or were there occasions when it all passed you by? How did you feel about the tests? It's important to do this analysis, since you can seek feedback from the company if you are unsuccessful and you will want to compare their comments with your own feelings.

 Activity 12.3

Get your assessment programme and list all the activities down one side of the page. Now think about what happened and rate yourself on a scale of 1 – 5 for each activity. Where your rating is low, make some notes about what you did and what you could do better.

If you're not successful, try ringing the Graduate Recruitment Office as soon as you receive your letter. If they're not too busy, they may talk to you individually about your performance. However, they often are extremely busy during the selection season and they may ask you to put your request in writing. Ask for specific reasons for your rejection and for feedback on test results as well as general comments on your performance at the assessment centre.

Activity 12.4

It may be useful now to write down a plan of action for future occasions. I've given a short example here, but you will need to make your own when the need arises.

Feedback (self or company)	Action
	• Careers Service test sessions? • Find some reference books on aptitude tests. • Find some basic school arithmetic test books.
	• Careers Service workshop? • Watch AGCAS video *Two whole days.*
	• More information about job. • Fix up work experience. • Talk to people doing the job.

Remember that your performance will improve with practice, so any apparent weaknesses at your first assessment centre may very well have disappeared by the time you reach your third!

Summary

If you are invited to the assessment centre, you are already successful. You have reached the last 5 per cent, and companies are definitely interested in you. Look forward to these days as an enjoyable challenge.

Even if it doesn't work out first time, you are well on the way to your first graduate job and, with some careful thought and extra preparation, next time could bring the longed-for letter.

Dear Mark,

I am delighted to be able to offer you . . . . .

Well done! Now wasn't it all worthwhile?

'Advice – just try to relax and be yourself. Be friendly. Everyone else feels nervous as well, so just make the effort and you'll feel a lot better. I know I did. I must have done OK – I got the job.'

13 Bibliography

Barrett, J. and Williams, G. (1990) *Test your own aptitude*, London, Kogan Page.

Bryon, M. (1994) *Graduate recruitment tests*, London, Kogan Page.

Bryon, M. and Modha, S. (1992) *How to master selection tests*, London, Kogan Page.

Eastwood, J. (1993) *Presentation skills*, Leicester, De Montfort University .

Eysenck, H. and Wilson, G. (1991) *Know your own personality*, Harmondsworth, Penguin.

Eysenck, H. (1990) *Know your own IQ*, Harmondsworth, Penguin.

Company information

The following sources may be available in your university library or in the business section of a large public library:

Extel Cards (Extel Financial Ltd)
McCarthy Cards, UK (McCarthy Information Ltd)
The Hambro Company Guide (Hemmington Scott Publishing)
Kelly's Business Directory (Reed Information Services)
Key British Enterprises (Dun & Bradstreet)
Kompass UK (Reed Information Services)
Who Owns Whom (Dun & Bradstreet)

Careers Advisory Service resources

Your Careers Advisory Service holds a great deal of information about self-assessment and job hunting, much of which is produced by AGCAS (The Association of Graduate Careers Advisory Services). The following material is particularly relevant:

Applications and interviews. A very useful book containing hints on preparation for first- and second-stage interviews.

Two whole days. The second stage – assessment centre. (20 minute video.)

Check with your Careers Advisory Service about the availability of second interview workshops and aptitude testing sessions.

Appendix: Aptitude test answers

Example A: Verbal reasoning

a A – this is clearly true as the passage states that only 30 per cent of drivers breath-tested were completely alcohol-free, consequently 70 per cent had taken alcohol.

b A – again clearly true. The passage states that the drink-driving record of married drivers is better (50 per cent alcohol-free) than that of the general population sample (30 per cent alcohol-free).

c C – cannot say/insufficient evidence. The passage does not state what proportion of the sample were unmarried, therefore you cannot substantiate this statement.

One important message for this type of verbal reasoning test is that you must base your answers *solely* on the information provided. Don't bring your own knowledge or assumptions into your answers. You are being tested on how well you can interpret and reason with data, not on what you know about the subject.

Example B: Quantitative reasoning

a 3. This is a given number.

b 13. This is the sum of the cars with only stereo cassettes (5) and those with stereo and automatic transmission (8). Don't forget to include these 8 as the question does not ask for those with only a stereo cassette.

c 6. The total number of cars is 42. The given numbers add up to 27, therefore the three question marks add up to 15. 17 cars have two refinements, therefore the two question marks where two circles overlap equals 9, because we are given the other equals 8. Therefore the middle question mark where all three circles overlap equals 6 (15 – 9).

You can solve this without knowing the individual values of the other two question marks.

Example C: Non-verbal/diagrammatic reasoning

The missing figure is **b**. Reasoning is as follows:

- Both the given figures have one shape within another shape (triangle in circle, circle in square), therefore the remaining combination is square and triangle.
- Both the figures have a smaller version of the enclosed shape at one end.
- Both the figures have the following pattern ⊢⊣ at the other end.

b is the only figure which combines these features.

102

Example D

a 4 – just and blonde equate to fair

b 5 – loud and hard are the opposite of soft

c 1 – letter, word, sentence, *paragraph*, page, chapter, book

d 1.4 – 2 x .7 = 1.4

e 5 – hear is to see as listen is to look

f 5 – backwards is to reversed as upside-down is to inverted

g 7/8 – pattern recognition – 1/2 (2/3) 3/4 (5/4) 5/6 (7/6) 7/8
          The bracketed numbers are irrelevant.

h 24 – 6 (x2) 12 (x2) 24 (x2) 48 (x2) 96

Also available from Kogan Page